HEALING DEVOTIONAL FOR WOMEN

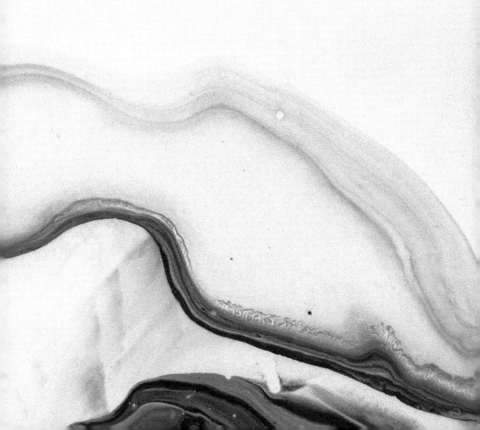

HEALING DEVOTIONAL FOR WOMEN

DAILY CHRISTIAN INSPIRATION FOR STRENGTH AND PEACE

REBECCA HASTINGS

ROCKRIDGE
PRESS

Interior and Cover Designer: Brieanna Felschow
Art Producer: Melissa Malinowsky
Editor: Adrian Potts
Production Editor: Jax Berman
Production Manager: Jose Olivera

All images used under license from Shutterstock. Author photo courtesy of Abigail Scott Photography

Paperback ISBN: 978-1-63807-211-9
eBook ISBN: 978-1-63807-626-1
R0

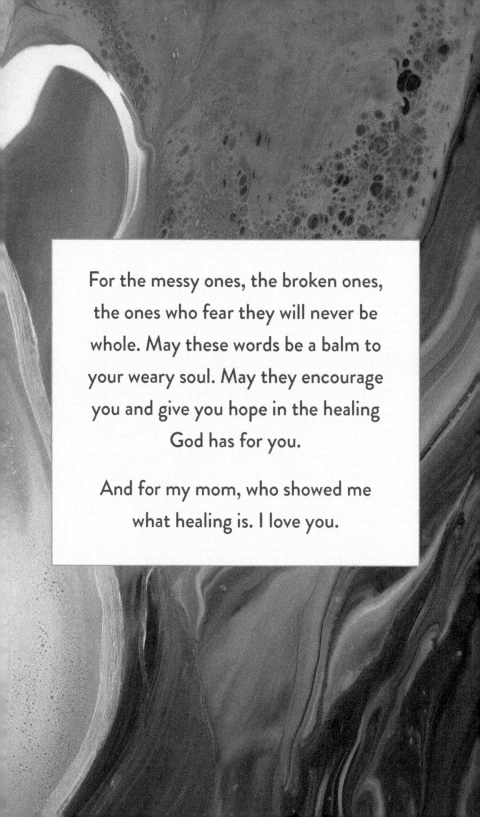

For the messy ones, the broken ones, the ones who fear they will never be whole. May these words be a balm to your weary soul. May they encourage you and give you hope in the healing God has for you.

And for my mom, who showed me what healing is. I love you.

CONTENTS

PART TWO: START TO HEAL

INTRODUCTION

Friend, I'm so glad you're here. I know we just met, but we are about to go on a journey together to a place of deeper healing and hope in your life. Whether you are carrying anxiety, sadness, or relationship woes; whether it's about something that happened long ago or yesterday; whether it's a wound that goes deep or a spiritual uplift for your soul—you are in the right place.

How can I possibly know that? Because I've been through these things, too. I've experienced abandonment and loss. I've walked through fear and mistrust. I've had days when I needed to feel a renewed sense of God deep inside me. And I have seen God heal things I never thought possible.

This book is for us. The ones who are longing for healing and freedom in our souls. As you go through these pages, you can hear the invitation whispered with each word, each scripture, each prayer: "Will you let God heal you?"

There is no competition in this space. You are invited to come with whatever you need healed. It doesn't matter how big or how small it is. These pages are for you.

The first section of this book will help you connect (or reconnect) with God. It's a foundation we are laying, one page at a time, to help you fully understand who God is, how much He loves you, and the healing He has for you. Consider this section packing your bags for the journey.

The second section goes deeper. It is the forward motion on your journey, to take steps on your unique path of emotional healing. This is where you see the progress you are longing for. For some people, it makes sense to go through the book from beginning to end. For others, it may be a more selective journey, visiting the devotions that connect the most with what you need for that day. No matter how you choose to take the journey, two things are certain.

First, your journey is yours. It will look different from that of anyone else (and that's a good thing!). God wants to work with you, specifically on *your* hurts, worries, fears, or whatever emotional healing you need. As you go through these pages, you can't do it wrong or get all the answers right. Your job is simply to seek God and see what He wants to do in you. He is faithful to meet you right where you are.

Second, you will experience healing. God promises healing, not because of anything specific we do but because of who He is. Although it may not happen in a day, every time you choose to open this book, to pursue your healing and wholeness, God will be faithful to meet you. He will work in you with love and gentleness to heal the tender places in your soul.

This book is for you, and it will help guide you as you seek healing from the Lord. It's important to recognize that this is one tool, one piece of your journey toward healing. For some, it may be enough in this season. For others, more tools may be required. One of the best tools we have is help from professional counselors and doctors who can guide us in ways no book can. As you go through these pages, consider what tools you need in this season and look to the Resources (page 125) for further help. There is no shame in using the tools God gives us to experience the healing we long for.

As you work through these pages, my hope is that you don't rush. Take your time as you read the scriptures. Consider the stories. Pray the prayers, reflect on the questions, and try the practices suggested each day.

This book is yours—use it. Highlight and underline, answer the questions, and add your own prayers. Although it may be a devotional, this is *your* devotional, a journal of your journey toward healing. Use it well.

If you miss a day, don't worry. You're not off track or late. Trust that God will use each devotional at just the right time in your life. I am cheering for you, friend, but even more than that, God is cheering for you.

Listen carefully. Each day is an invitation directly from God's heart to yours. You are invited to live in hope and healing. Are you ready?

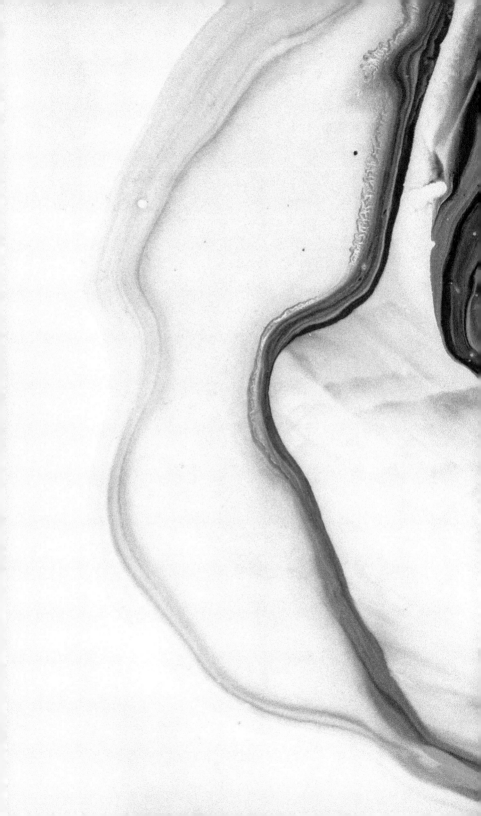

PART ONE

Turn to God

When things feel hard, the only thing we want is for them to feel better. We want a direct path to joy and peace and freedom. It's easy to get so focused on where we are (in the hard place) and where we want to be (in freedom) that we forget to look for the way to get there.

This first section is all about getting started on that path. In these devotions, you will discover the foundation you need for the healing you long for. Are you ready to walk in healing? Let's start by leaning on God.

God Is Ready for You

In the same way you received Jesus our Lord and
Messiah by faith, continue your journey of faith,
progressing further into your union with him! Your
spiritual roots go deeply into his life as you are
continually infused with strength, encouraged in every
way. For you are established in the faith you have
absorbed and enriched by your devotion to him!

—Colossians 2:6–7, TPT

I stood at the end of my driveway and looked left, then right. I had
already laced up my sneakers and gotten myself out the door, so there
was no doubt I was going for a walk. Now I faced a decision: Which
way was I going to go?

That's where you are right now. No, you may not actually have
sneakers laced, and you probably are not standing at the end of your
driveway, but you are facing a decision.

If you've picked up this book, you've decided you want healing. You
want to be free from the things you are struggling with, the things that
wear you down day after day. That's the getting ready part, the lacing
up your sneakers.

Now it's time to decide which way to go. If you go one way, you can
try to do this on your own, figuring out each twist and turn, hoping this
time will be better than last time. Hoping you'll get closer to the healing
you long for.

But if you go the other way, you can do this with Someone. You can
walk in step with Someone who loves you and will guide you, Someone

who will hold you up and cheer you on, and Someone who wants your healing even more than you do.

Do you want to try to do this on your own, or do you want to do this with God? This choice may seem too simple and obvious, but it's one of the most important decisions you'll make on this journey. You may even need to make it more than once. Choosing God matters.

Whether you feel close to God or far away, whether you've walked with Him for ten years or are just thinking about it for the first time, no matter what, God is ready to do this with you. You don't have to walk through your healing alone. You have a God who is longing to guide you, help you, and love you today.

You may have heard it said that God is gentle; He won't force Himself in. Instead, He waits, fully ready for you to come to Him, fully ready for you to ask for His help, and fully ready to walk with you on this journey toward freedom and peace and joy.

Are you ready? Let's go!

LET'S PRAY

God, I don't want to make this journey on my own. I choose to walk with You today and each day as I move forward in my healing. Amen.

When It Feels Exhausting

"Are you tired? Worn out? Burned out on religion? Come to me. Get away with me and you'll recover your life. I'll show you how to take a real rest. Walk with me and work with me—watch how I do it. Learn the unforced rhythms of grace. I won't lay anything heavy or ill-fitting on you. Keep company with me and you'll learn to live freely and lightly."

–Matthew 11:28–30, MSG

I have a foster puppy. He's adorable and lovable with his cute puppy face and soft puppy coat to snuggle and pet. It's funny to watch him play as he chases his toys or even his own tail. And then it's time for bed.

When the lights went out that first night, my cute foster puppy started whining. It wasn't too bad. And then his whine turned into a little howl. Soon that howl turned into a full-on song of howls, barks, and whines that made it impossible for anyone to get any rest. Needless to say, the next morning I was a bit tired.

We all know what it's like to feel tired in our body. We can take a nap or drink an extra cup of coffee. But what about when we feel tired deep in our soul? The tired that comes when we face a rejection that hurts us deeper than we care to admit; or when we carry worry around with us everywhere we go, never quite knowing how to put it down. Or even when we face a loss that knocks the wind out of us, and we wonder how we will keep breathing.

Maybe you've been carrying hard things no one even knows about—things you hold in, trying to keep it all together, worried that if you let anything out you will split wide open. All that holding in and holding tight can feel exhausting, leaving you tired and afraid it will always be this way.

What do we do when we feel soul weary from all the hard things we've been carrying?

In Matthew, when Jesus was teaching the crowds, He told us exactly what to do when our soul is weary: Come to Him. There is no disclaimer, no guideline, no rule. He simply tells us to come.

When we come, He offers us recovery, rest, and grace—the things our weary souls need to become whole and healthy.

What you're facing right now is a lot more complicated than lack of sleep because of a singing puppy. Jesus knew it would be, and He is ready for all of it.

LET'S REFLECT

What holds you back from bringing the hard things to Jesus?
How do you feel when you read Jesus's words in Matthew?
What part of the verses brings the most comfort?

Faithful in the Hard Places

She answered God by name, praying to the God who spoke to her, "You're the God who sees me! Yes! He saw me; and then I saw him!"

—Genesis 16:13, MSG

Do you know Hagar? Certainly not personally, since she lived around 1900 BC. So let me introduce you.

This woman lived a hard life. She was a slave and a concubine, used by Sarai to bear a child with Abram, Sarai's husband, since having a baby wasn't working out for Sarai. When Hagar did get pregnant, everyone was mad, and they let her know it. It's a hard and messy story full of injustice, prejudice, and heartache.

Maybe you can relate?

The story of an abused slave isn't the rosy place we usually look for God's faithfulness. But God often shows up in the places we least expect, that seem too messy for a holy God or too far from Him—the place where He showed up for Hagar.

When Hagar was pregnant, Abram wanted nothing to do with her and Sarai mistreated her, so Hagar ran away. But guess what God did: He sent an angel. He sent help, and more than that, He sent hope in the hard place. God didn't remove her from the situation. In fact, Hagar had to keep walking through the hard. But God did bring something she needed: presence.

God brought Hagar a reminder that she wasn't alone in that hard place. Hagar even said of God, "You're the God who sees me!"

Your hard place is different from Hagar's. Your life looks different, full of your unique worries and struggles. Although your circumstances are different, heartache and hardship are a universal language.

Just like Hagar, you may have places in your story that feel messy, full of injustice and heartache. Maybe you've even run away from the hard things, trying to escape their grip on you, feeling alone in the wilderness. But what if you could see that you are not alone at all? What if your wilderness, like Hagar's, is actually a perfect place to see God's faithfulness?

We all want a way out, but sometimes God doesn't remove us from the hard places. Instead, He shows His faithfulness to be present with us in those places. Just as He was for Hagar, God is the one who sees you. He shows up, fully present to comfort you, instruct you, and show His faithfulness to you.

LET'S PUT IT INTO PRACTICE

Look for God's faithfulness in your hard places. These don't have to be big things, like sending an angel. It may be something small, like an unexpected text from a friend or a special song on the radio. Think about two or three examples, and thank God for His faithfulness to you.

Will You Tell the Truth?

For God did not send his Son into the world
to condemn the world, but to save the
world through him.

–John 3:17

It was a bright, sunny day, and I was driving along by my town green. I had my three children strapped into their seats behind me, a perfectly ordinary day of caring for kids and running errands. My phone rang, and I groaned a bit when I realized my Bluetooth wasn't working. Without another thought, I picked up the phone and answered.

Sixty seconds later I saw the flashing lights behind me. In Connecticut, it's against the law to use a handheld cell phone while driving. Now I was being pulled over.

This was the first time I had ever been pulled over, so I was a bit flustered. When the police officer approached my window and asked if I was talking on a cell phone while driving, I had a choice. I could make something up, or I could tell the truth.

When it comes to our relationship with God, we have that same choice. We can try to cover up what's really going on in our hearts, painting pictures of how everything is fine, or we can get real. We can tell Him where we're really at, what we're feeling, and the things that are going on in our hearts.

Just like that police officer, God already knows what's going on. But unlike that police officer, He sees into our hearts; He knows what we're thinking. Still, He gives us the choice about how real we are willing to be. Why? It's part of being in a relationship with someone. And God longs for a relationship with us.

You get to choose. Will you tell God what you're really feeling, thinking, and struggling with, or will you gloss over things, trying to make light of them? Are you willing to go deep with God, sharing even the hardest things—the questions and the worries? What kind of relationship do you want with God?

Unlike my experience with that police officer, God doesn't have a ticket all queued up and ready for you. He is not waiting to catch you in a mistake. But He does give you a choice. Being real with God allows you to stop covering up the hard things and instead walk through them with His help.

The heart of God is never to condemn you; it is always to offer grace when you come to Him. He welcomes you with love every single time.

LET'S PRAY

Lord, sometimes it's hard for me to be real with You. I pretend things are okay or avoid coming to You. Help me share my full heart with You today. Amen.

When Feelings Spiral Out of Control

Then Jesus told them this parable: "Suppose one of you has a hundred sheep and loses one of them. Doesn't he leave the ninety-nine in the open country and go after the lost sheep until he finds it?"

–Luke 15:3–4

I don't usually think of myself as a sheep, but Jesus liked to use stories and imagery to teach us things. One of the most famous of His metaphors is sheep. In Luke, Jesus talks about a shepherd with 99 sheep who followed the rules and one sheep who wandered off the path.

It's easy to relate to this singular sheep, wandering off and ending up all alone in a bit of a situation. Maybe she was just lost in a different field. But more likely the story from Luke is talking about a sheep in need of rescue—a sheep who went astray and was now in a hard situation, away from the safety and care of the shepherd. Even in this, Jesus reminds us that the shepherd leaves all the other sheep in their safe place just to find that one who went off track.

I have a tendency to spiral. I did it just the other day, getting mad about some little thing that happened with my husband, then the dog wouldn't listen, then I stubbed my toe. I lost it. I was upset, and I made sure everyone around me knew it.

When things are overwhelming and my emotions get the best of me, one hard thing leads to another, to another. Before I know it, I have spiraled into a pit that feels impossible to get out of. The worst part is, it's usually my own doing.

Sometimes it's because my emotions are haywire from hormones and all my big feelings. Other times it's because I've been keeping in a million little feelings, and they build up so much I can't help but let them out all at once. Honestly, saying "let them out" feels kind. It's more of a volcano.

The hardest thing for me when I'm in this place is when my husband pulls me into a hug. Feeling loved when I am standing in a mess of my own doing isn't easy. It seems to go against everything I think I deserve in that moment. But love is one of the best ways out of a pit.

Jesus does that for you, too. When things get off track, when feelings are big and life seems messy, Jesus, the good shepherd, stops everything to come for you in love.

LET'S PRAY

God, thank you for being my good shepherd. You always come for me, even when things feel so messy and I am lost in my feelings. Show me Your love and faithfulness in my hard places. Amen.

The Truth about Surrender

Those who know your name trust in you, for you, Lord,
have never forsaken those who seek you.

–Psalm 9:10

After having a serious car accident my senior year of college, I missed
a month of classes. I still remember sitting across from my advisor,
him resting his elbows on his desk and tenting his fingers as he said I
needed to drop the semester. He said I had missed too much work and
could never catch up.

Challenge accepted.

I wasn't going to give up. I was determined to prove him wrong,
and I set out to get the work done. But recovering from an accident,
maintaining my current studies, and catching up with what I missed
ended up being more than I could handle. I could feel myself teetering
on the edge of giving up, and I felt like a failure. In desperation, I told
God I needed His help. I surrendered my plans, my work, and even my
timetable to God. Even if it meant I wouldn't graduate on time.

But I still didn't give up. I kept working, offering it to God each step
of the way. I wasn't sure I would get it all done, but something shifted in
me when I remembered that I could trust God in that place where I felt
so inadequate.

For so long, I had thought of giving up and surrendering as the
same thing. I had this idea in my head that surrender equaled weakness and lack of ability. But I was completely off base. When I let go of
the things I couldn't control and offered it all to God, when I went to
God honestly, surrender felt like an exhale. I had no idea that surrender
would turn out to be my greatest strength in getting my work done.

So often we look at surrender as weakness, a kind of failure. But God calls us to surrender, to get real and let go of all the false ideas we hold on to so tightly, hoping they will get us through. He wants us to be completely honest about who we are and, even more, honest about who He is.

When our eyes are fixed on ourselves, surrender looks like giving up. But when our eyes are fixed on God, surrender is all about depending on Him. We can surrender to God because He is infinitely stronger than we could ever be. It's in this place that we can trust what the Psalm says about Him: God does not forsake us, ever.

The idea of surrender can feel challenging when it comes to our healing. We think we need to figure it all out and do the work by ourselves. God wants something better for us. Surrender is all about putting God first so we can walk forward trusting Him. Are you ready to surrender today?

LET'S REFLECT

What do you think about when you hear the word *surrender*? Does surrender feel like a weakness or a relief? What is one thing about God that makes the idea of surrender feel good?

Remember to Go to God

For we do not have a high priest who is unable to empathize with our weaknesses, but we have one who has been tempted in every way, just as we are—yet he did not sin. Let us then approach God's throne of grace with confidence, so that we may receive mercy and find grace to help us in our time of need.

–Hebrews 4:15–16

My teenage daughter and I had just had a discussion that ended with her in her room and me in mine. I closed the door behind me hoping for a little bit of privacy. There may still have been steam coming out my ears.

I reached for my phone and clicked my mom's number before I even knew what I was going to say. I needed someone to listen, someone who could understand.

When my mom answered on the third ring, I let out a sigh. I didn't even know where to begin. I didn't want to argue with my daughter. My mom would understand. So I told her everything. I poured it out, probably with some embellishment: the disagreement, the frustration, the tears. I told her I didn't know what to do.

Mom listened well, responding gently at all the right moments. She was on my team. She understood. And then she said, "Have you prayed about it?"

Ugh! Why did she have to go there? I didn't want to pray. I wanted a real-life person to talk to. Someone who understood. Someone who wouldn't make me wait for an answer or guess what to do.

I let out a sigh. "No, Mom."

She could sense my frustration, but she encouraged me to try. We finished our call, and I lay on my bed. And I talked to God. I even told Him that I didn't want to talk to Him because I wanted a real person who understood me.

Then I remembered: He does understand.

Jesus went through pain and heartache, rejection and loss, struggle and pressure. The circumstances of His experiences were different, but the emotional struggle was the same, even the same as my argument with my teen.

The book of Hebrews reminds us of God's ability to empathize with us. Writing during a time of great persecution, the writer is clear that Jesus was tempted in every way and, therefore, is fully able to relate to us. Our job is to "approach God's throne of grace with confidence, so that we may receive mercy and find grace to help us in our time of need."

When something goes wrong—when your feelings are all over the place and you need someone to talk to—it is wonderful to have trusted people to go to. But we should never let those people be a replacement for going to God. We can bring Him all our feelings in prayer, fully confident that He will meet us with mercy and grace when we need it most.

LET'S PUT IT INTO PRACTICE

The next time you are struggling and pick up the phone to share with someone, take a minute to first talk to God about your feelings.

When We Laugh at God

Now the Lord was gracious to Sarah as he had said,
and the Lord did for Sarah what he had promised.
Sarah became pregnant and bore a son to Abraham in
his old age, at the very time God had promised him.

—Genesis 21:1–2

Has someone ever said something really absurd to you? Something that would be impossible? So absurd and impossible that it made you laugh?

Sarah, in the Bible, did just that.

She didn't have the most stellar record of faith. You may remember her from Hagar's story. Sarah's name then was Sarai, and she was the one who made Hagar bear a child with her own husband. Things were kind of a mess.

Thirteen years later things got really strange. When Sarai was around 90 years old, God formed a covenant with her husband and changed their names. We don't know a lot about what happened or why, but Sarai became Sarah. And that's not all that changed.

God promised them a baby. This barren older woman—the one who was so desperate with longing that she offered her slave to her husband just so they could have a baby. The one who mistreated Hagar so badly that Hagar ran away. Sarah overheard a conversation between the Lord and her husband that she was going to have the very thing she had longed for her whole marriage. A baby. At 90. Can you imagine?

Sarah did what any of us would do: She laughed. But God isn't one to make jokes like that. And sure enough, Sarah did have a baby the following year.

Sometimes I laugh at God's promises—maybe not aloud, but in my heart. When I read things about His promises for healing, for example, it feels so completely impossible that something in me laughs at the absurdity.

But God is always faithful. He is a God who keeps His promises. Instead of laughing at them, or brushing them aside and thinking they are for someone else, what if we believed them? What if, instead of laughing like Sarah did, we chose to trust even when it doesn't make sense?

The Bible is full of stories that don't make sense. A whole nation in slavery is brought to freedom. A Jewish woman marries the king and saves her people. A laughing 90-year-old woman has a baby. Instead of looking for what makes sense, we are invited into faith to see what God does.

Promises and faithfulness matter to God. God keeps His promises. He did then and He does now. You can trust God because He keeps His promises to you. Always.

LET'S REFLECT

What promises from God do you laugh at? Which ones seem impossible to you? How can you choose to believe God's promises in those places?

When Your Struggle Seems Unimportant

Look to the Lord and his strength;
seek his face always.

–1 Chronicles 16:11

I stood there completely naked, reached back, and pulled the ponytail elastic out of my hair. I wanted nothing extra. I thought about taking off my wedding ring but finally decided I was being ridiculous. Then I stepped on the scale.

The digital display was working, thinking, processing the weight of me on a 12-by-12 square. It took only seconds for the scale to measure me.

Standing there in the early morning, naked and cold, I couldn't help but wonder: Is this who I am? Am I a number? Am I too much? Am I a failure?

My struggle with weight has been part of my life as long as I can remember. I hate that it is. I know all the things we talk about with #BodyPositivity and #YourBodyIsGood. But still I struggle. It's a hard place I walk in daily, and I do it alone.

I have plenty of other hard places. But this is one I can't seem to get through, no matter what I do. And even as I write this, I'm noticing one thing: "I." *I* keep trying. *I* can't do it. *I* wish it were different.

The truth is, I will never do this on my own. The only way to move through our hard places and find the freedom on the other side is by opening the doors to God.

What hard places do you walk through alone?

Maybe you're like me, struggling with your weight; maybe it's a loss you can't find your way out of or a relationship that isn't what you thought it would be; maybe it's your work or the dreams you can't seem to make happen.

Whatever your hard place is, walking through it on your own is difficult and lonely. God wants to walk with you in your hard places, especially the ones you keep hidden. He longs to be there for you, guiding you and comforting you as you go through each day. He is ready with the strength you need.

Asking for His help doesn't always feel easy. With my struggle with weight, it even feels silly, as if it's too inconsequential to bother God about.

When King David is instructing his leaders in today's verse, he reminds them how important it is to seek God in all they face. He doesn't give guidelines for what things are too small or what things are too personal. He reminds them to seek the Lord's strength always.

We can remember this today and seek God in everything we face.

LET'S PUT IT INTO PRACTICE

Think about one hard thing you're struggling with, even if it seems small or unimportant. Ask God to come and help you in your struggle today.

When You Take a Hard Fall

No need to panic over alarms or surprises,
or predictions that doomsday's just around the
corner, Because God will be right there with you;
he'll keep you safe and sound.

–Proverbs 3:25–26, MSG

The blood hadn't even dried. I'm not sure the tears had, either. Just minutes before, my daughter was racing her bike around the pavement as fast as she could. We'd gone to the big empty parking lot at the high school so the kids could have more room to ride. She loved the extra space, but even more than that, she loved the extra speed. The parking lot gave her the room she needed to go full out, as fast as her little legs could spin.

One wrong move changed everything—a turn taken a bit too fast, maybe with a handful of gravel in the wrong place, and she wiped out. Her leg and hands took the brunt of it, blood and tears both flowing freely.

Naturally, I scooped her up to assess the damage and comfort her. We got the first aid kit from the car and bandaged everything the best we could. When I asked if she wanted to go home, she sniffled and shook her head. She wanted to stay. She wanted to try again. I hesitated for a moment and then said okay, reminding her I'd be right there with her.

Isn't God just like that with us? When we take a fall or push through something uncomfortable, we can come to Him to patch us up. We can keep going, trusting that He stands there at the ready, offering His presence and help.

My daughter trusted me to help her. And she was confident I would keep helping her if she needed me. She got back on that bike and kept going.

It wasn't because her fall didn't hurt. And it wasn't because she wanted it to happen again. She was able to get up and keep going because she trusted that she wouldn't face anything alone. She knew I would be there to watch her, to cheer her on, and to help her if she got hurt. Sure, there was some determination and grit mixed in as well, but the thing that helped her keep going was confidence that I would be there.

We can have that same confidence in God. As we walk through our healing, as we face hard and messy things, we can trust that God is there watching us, cheering us on, helping us, and caring for us if we get hurt. We can be confident that He is there for us every step of the way.

LET'S PRAY

Father, no matter what I face today, help me come to you, confident that you will help me in my time of need. I trust you to be there for me in grace and mercy. Amen.

Shift Your Focus

But I will not take my love from him, nor will I ever
betray my faithfulness.

–Psalm 89:33

Do you believe God loves you and never betrays His faithfulness?
When life is going well, it's easy to nod and say, "Yes, absolutely." But
what about when things feel really awful? Do you believe that same
love and faithfulness in the hardest moments?

I passed out the other day. This isn't all that uncommon for me.
I've passed out in my bedroom, at the gym, and even once when I was
driving. That last time was the worst, for obvious reasons. But despite
a terrible accident involving the jaws of life, my injuries were minor, I
didn't hurt anyone else, and I went home the same day.

They discovered a few things about my body after my accident. I
have a heart condition, and I have epilepsy. Doctors don't know which
one causes me to pass out, but we work hard to prevent it.

On this particular day, I had donated blood. Donating never made
me pass out before, but this time it did. And it felt awful. Every time
feels awful. Unfortunate things can happen, like peeing or vomiting.
Never mind the obvious risks like injury—simply put, it's terrible. My
body takes some time to reset.

It's easy to lose sight of God's faithfulness when something feels so
miserable and scary. When I look at the obvious, all I see is my terrify-
ing experience, the pain, the embarrassment, the fear. In those things, I
can't seem to see God.

But when I stop looking at all the feelings and instead look for evidence, I find Him every single time.

This particular day when I donated blood, I wasn't alone. My husband happened to be there. I didn't fall and hit my head; I miraculously
stayed in the chair. The woman in charge was so kind and knew how

to help. And my husband, a nurse and paramedic, was able to call his coworkers at the firehouse, who came to assist.

Do you see the shift? When we shift our eyes from all the emotions and consciously look for evidence of God's faithfulness, it's right there. Honestly, it makes me smile when I think about that day.

Was it awful? Absolutely. But can I see how faithful God was to me? You bet I can.

God doesn't need to *show up*. He is always there. He doesn't need to *try* to be faithful. He is always faithful. All we need to do is shift how we look at things, and we will see Him.

LET'S REFLECT

What is something hard you walked through recently? What did it feel like? Where can you see evidence of God's faithfulness in that hard situation?

Do You Really Know Love?

"For the mountains may depart and the hills be removed, but my steadfast love shall not depart from you, and my covenant of peace shall not be removed," says the Lord, who has compassion on you.

−Isaiah 54:10, ESV

There are so many things I want my son to know. I want him to know how to do his laundry and cook a nice meal. I want him to know that kindness matters and that grades don't define him. I want him to know who he is. I want him to be confident in that.

But most of all I want him to know love.

No matter how many things I want him to learn, no matter what I think is important or even essential to lead a healthy and happy life, no matter how much he gets wrong or right in his life, I want him to know true love. And I'm not talking about romantic love.

I mean love that is unconditional and full and deep, love that is endless and dependable and sees through all the messy places, no matter how messy they are. I want him to know love deep in every cell of his body.

If I am a human—a flawed, mortal being—and I want this deep love for my son, what do you think God wants for you?

It's easy to breeze past the idea of God's love for us; to nod politely and turn the page because it seems so basic, like a Sunday school lesson on repeat. Even the song feels basic: "Jesus loves me, this I know…"

But if God's love for us is so simple, why do we struggle to believe it? To trust it deep in our core?

I get so caught up in knowing myself, with all my flaws, that it's easy to dismiss the Sunday school version of God's love. It's easy to think, "Yeah, He loves me, but . . ." and then walk through life grasping only a fraction of the love God has for me.

God's love isn't a Sunday school lesson, and it's not something that changes with whether or not you accept it.

God's love for you is complete, full, and endless.

It doesn't depend on anything else, good or bad.

God's love for you is bigger than your understanding of it. Look at the words used in Isaiah about His love: *steadfast* and *will not depart*. The love He offers to comfort and reassure Israel is the same love He has for you. And He longs to show you more of that love today!

LET'S PUT IT INTO PRACTICE

Read today's verse aloud, and declare God's steadfast love for you!

When Waiting Feels Hard

Wait for the Lord; be strong, and let your heart take courage; wait for the Lord!

—Psalm 27:14, ESV

Waiting is hard. No matter how much you understand why you have to wait, whether you've been waiting for a few minutes or a few decades, waiting brings up so many feelings. As much as you try to apply logic, the feelings that come with waiting are not easy.

You understand why you're not quickly moving up the ladder at work, but waiting your turn feels like torture. Watching every friend you have get married is exciting, but wondering when it will be your turn feels lonely. Moving forward with life feels great, but continuing to carry around old hurts feels exhausting.

The Bible tells us a lot about waiting. My favorite verses about waiting are always from the people who really understand that unique longing in the soul that comes with waiting. Anna knew all about waiting.

After only seven years of marriage, Anna became a widow. Although she was perceived to be young and could have looked for a new husband, she chose to spend her life in the Temple. There, she spent her days worshiping, fasting, and praying, talking often about the baby that would come and change the world. This was her life. It wasn't the one she had originally planned, but she shifted gears and made something new.

Anna knew waiting. She wasn't waiting for a husband. She wasn't waiting for a new vocation. Anna was waiting to meet the baby Jesus. Even before He was born, she waited.

The Bible tells us she was 84 years old when Mary and Joseph brought the baby Jesus to the Temple. Anna waited *decades* to see the one thing her heart longed for. We don't know her prayers or what she was thinking during those years, but it's not hard to imagine the mix of hope and weariness that comes in the waiting seasons. It's not hard to imagine because we can relate.

Although Anna's prayers are not recorded in scripture, there are so many examples in the Psalms of David calling out for God's help and declaring His truth in seasons of waiting.

From deep inside, David cried out and declared hope in his waiting: "Out of the depths I cry to you, Lord [. . .] I wait for the Lord, my whole being waits" (Psalm 130:1, 5, NIV).

Sometimes David even begged God when waiting felt hard. "Please, Lord! Come quickly and rescue me!" (Psalm 40:13, TPT).

And when David felt surrounded by adversaries, when he was weary and longed for his waiting to end, he told us, "Wait for the Lord; be strong, and let your heart take courage; wait for the Lord!"

No matter how hard the waiting is—no matter how long it takes or how desperate we feel—we can bring it to God, taking courage and finding strength as we wait for the Lord.

LET'S PRAY

Lord, sometimes waiting feels hard and lonely. Give me the courage I need to wait, and remind me of Your presence in this place. Amen.

You Don't Need to Have the Plan

I know what I'm doing. I have it all planned out—plans
to take care of you, not abandon you, plans to give you
the future you hope for.

–Jeremiah 29:11, MSG

One summer we went on a family vacation that involved a big amusement park. My youngest was around nine, and she was having a great time, but she was a little leery of the roller coasters. She wanted to go on them, but her fear was holding her back.

After what felt like hours of looking at the map and walking around, she found one that looked small. She felt like she could do it, so she made a plan. When we returned to the park the following day, she would go on a roller coaster named the Verbolten; in fact, we would all go on it.

Walking up to the ride, I agreed that it looked like a great starter coaster. The track curved and didn't have a big drop. At least, not that we could see from the entrance. We strapped in and waited with anticipation for the ride to start.

Let's just say we were wrong about the ride—very, very wrong. The majority of it was not visible from the entrance. Not only did it have all the typical coaster features, but there was a dark tunnel and a sudden drop straight down in the pitch black. It was not what we had planned.

The truth is, I love a great plan. When everything is laid out and I know what to expect today and in the days to come, I am happy. One of my favorite things is filling out a calendar or a new planner. Even looking at a big map that shows the exact route and any side routes I might need to get to my destination makes me happy.

It feels safe.

When life goes according to plan, I don't worry that the floor is about to drop out from under me—but life is a lot like that roller coaster. We see part of the ride. We have an idea of what to expect. However, the specifics don't always follow the plan we made.

Sometimes it feels like the floor drops out. Sometimes it feels like we are plunging into darkness. And a lot of times we think, *This is not what I signed up for.*

But God made the ride. He sees the whole map. He has the blueprints. Much to my dismay, He doesn't just hand them over to us. But He does promise that He sees the whole ride, and He will always be strapped right in with us.

When we remember who God is, we can trust His plans and presence in our lives, even when we can't see them.

LET'S REFLECT

Do you prefer to have a plan, or do you feel comfortable when things are unknown? How do you feel when you are reminded that God has the plan and is present with you, no matter what happens?

A Sliver of Faith

But Jesus kept looking around to see who had done it.
Then the woman, knowing what had happened to her,
came and fell at his feet and, trembling with fear, told
him the whole truth. He said to her, "Daughter, your
faith has healed you. Go in peace and be freed from
your suffering."

–*Mark 5:32–34*

I've always been amazed by the story in the Bible of the bleeding woman. This unnamed woman had been hemorrhaging for twelve years—twelve years of bleeding, twelve years of seeking help and longing for it to end, twelve years of desperation and hope.

Enter Jesus.

He was walking around, as He often did, and a crowd gathered around Him. It wasn't just a few people; Mark describes the scene as people pressing in against Him. So many people wanted to be close to Him.

Our friend, the woman who was bleeding, was so desperate, but there was something else in her: a sliver of faith. She pressed into the crowd with everyone else, her sole intention to touch the hem of His cloak. You can picture it, frayed from dragging on the dusty ground.

Jesus was not even aware His cloak was dragging as He helped and taught the crowd of people. But she pressed in behind him and reached out her hand with the hope and faith that just touching His clothes would be enough to heal her of this affliction she had carried for over a decade.

There was no desire in her to talk to Him. No pressure to make a scene. She simply wanted to be invisible and experience healing from Jesus. But Jesus knew. The second she touched Him, probably even before that, He knew she had reached out in faith. Jesus felt power leave Him, and she was healed.

But this is where it gets interesting. Jesus didn't let her stay invisible. He wanted her to know that He saw her. He looked around to see who had touched him. When no one answered, He asked again, and "Then the woman, knowing what had happened to her, came and fell at his feet and, trembling with fear, told him the whole truth."

In the most beautiful way, Jesus had her come forward, and He spoke love and blessing over her.

God wants to do the same for us. As we reach out for our healing, a sliver of faith urging us to touch the hem of His cloak, He wants that moment with us. He wants to look us in the eyes and listen to the whole truth of why we have reached for Him. And He is ready to show us love and bless us as we walk in freedom.

He is looking for you in the crowd. Will you reach out in faith?

LET'S PUT IT INTO PRACTICE

Tell Jesus the whole truth today. Look in His eyes, and tell Him why you're here and the healing you long for in Him. Today is the day to reach out to your Savior.

PART TWO

Start to Heal

As we stand on the firm foundation of God, we are prepared for the work ahead. And it will be work. But we do not do the work alone.

The remaining devotions are about how we walk through healing together with God. Sorrow, fear, worry, anger, bitterness— whatever you seek freedom from can be healed in these pages. You need three things: your honest heart, God's truth, and to do the next thing. Don't look at the whole book; just look at the next thing God has for you today.

It All Hurts

Blessed be the God and Father of our Lord Jesus
Christ, the Father of mercies and God of all comfort,
who comforts us in all our affliction, so that we may
be able to comfort those who are in any affliction,
with the comfort with which we ourselves are
comforted by God.

–2 Corinthians 1:3–4, ESV

You may be experiencing a relationship breakdown, grieving the loss
of a loved one, coming to terms with past trauma, feeling overwhelmed
by the responsibilities of motherhood, facing fertility challenges,
coping with worry and sadness, struggling with body image issues, or
any number of these and other difficult situations.

It's easy to think of everyone's experiences as unique—and of
course, in many ways they are. But most of our experiences can be
sorted into just a few categories. The two most prominent are love and
pain. I know that seems simple. I know you'll think of things in your
own life that don't seem linked to either. But what about the ones that
do? What about the vast majority of experiences that you could quickly
sort into the love category or the pain category?

Think about the things you're feeling in your life, and let's just
sort them.

Job: Love or pain?

Relationships: Love or pain?

Faith, jeans size, sleep: Love or pain?

Do you have anything in the pain category? I know I do. And
honestly, the number of things in each category never seems to matter.
I could have 20 things in the love category and one thing in the pain
category. Still, that one thing would outweigh the 20.

That's how pain can be. When one thing hurts, everything else can feel like it hurts, too. It's as if the scales are miscalibrated and we can't seem to find a way to adjust them. Sometimes one hard, painful thing can make it feel like everything hurts.

And that's okay.

That's probably not what you expected to read. Usually, this is where the devotion would have an inspiring quote urging you to focus on the good, or some neat little bow to tie everything up with and make it feel simple and pretty. That's not why we're here.

We're here for healing. Healing, like pain, isn't always simple and rarely looks pretty every step of the way. Sometimes the first step in that process is just sorting through what's here without fixing it.

We can look at that one thing that hurts and recognize that it feels like everything hurts. We don't need to frantically search for the solution. We can exist right here and just recognize our pain.

LET'S REFLECT

What do your love/pain categories look like? Do you have things in the pain category that feel all encompassing? How does it feel to recognize that without trying to fix it?

Is Anyone Listening?

And you, my son Solomon, acknowledge the God of your father, and serve him with wholehearted devotion and with a willing mind, for the Lord searches every heart and understands every desire and every thought.

–1 Chronicles 28:9

You've likely seen this scene in a movie: There's a room full of people. They're all busy talking to one another, doing things, making noise. Maybe it's a party. Maybe there's music. And then you see the single person who needs to get everyone's attention.

For a moment or two, she looks around, trying to figure out how she's going to get everyone to hear her and stop what they're doing. She tries to say, "Everyone? Hello?" But no one can hear her. She says it again, a little louder, but still everything around her keeps going. She scans the room wondering how she will get everyone to be quiet. Finally, she summons some inner strength, puts her thumb and forefinger together, and uses them to whistle so loud everyone stops what they're doing.

I can relate to this woman—except I don't know how to whistle like that. Instead, I stand there in the crowd, looking around, wondering how I'm going to get people to listen.

When we are looking at our brokenness, sometimes we know we need help. But looking around, we feel like that woman staring at a room full of people living their happy, noisy lives. We feel like everyone else is busy, and we have no way to get their attention to even ask for help—especially when we don't know how to whistle.

God doesn't need us to whistle. He doesn't even need us to whisper. We can silently tell Him we need His help, and He's listening.

King David reminds us of this when he is commissioning and instructing his son Solomon: "And you, my son Solomon, acknowledge the God of your father, and serve him with wholehearted devotion and with a willing mind, for the Lord searches every heart and understands every desire and every thought."

Sometimes our attempts to ask for help can feel like a whisper that gets lost in the busyness of everyone else living their lives. But when we ask God, we never have to wonder if He is listening. We never have to figure out how to get His attention. We can hold on to the same reminder King David gave his son.

When it feels like no one is listening, like life is too busy, we can ask God for help with full confidence that He is present and will listen to us when we ask for His help. "The Lord searches every heart and understands every desire and every thought." And that includes yours.

LET'S PUT IT INTO PRACTICE

No matter what busyness is going on around you, ask God for His help with whatever you need today.

No One Understands

But to Jonah this seemed very wrong, and he became
angry. He prayed to the Lord, "Isn't this what I said,
Lord, when I was still at home? That is what I tried
to forestall by fleeing to Tarshish. I knew that you
are a gracious and compassionate God, slow to
anger and abounding in love, a God who relents from
sending calamity."

–Jonah 4:1–2

Remember Jonah in the Bible? He was the one who spent a few days in
the belly of a whale—yes, really. That may seem far fetched to us, but
considering some of the other things that happened in Bible days, a
little time-out inside a whale isn't so crazy.

We usually focus on what happened immediately before and
during the whale situation: how God told Jonah to go preach to the
people of Nineveh because they were a mess, how Jonah ran away on
a boat to avoid it and ended up inside the whale, and how Jonah turned
back to God and listened.

But his story doesn't end there. Jonah followed through, and so
did God. Jonah went to the people of Nineveh, and in a shocking turn
of events, they changed their ways. In fact, God didn't even bring the
destruction on the people of Nineveh that He had talked about. And
Jonah didn't like that. It didn't seem fair. Jonah thought he had every
right to be angry with God.

Sometimes I think I have a right to be angry with God. When life
is good, I don't feel that way. But it just doesn't seem fair that I am
struggling with my epilepsy or that I still grapple with feelings from my
biological father leaving us. It seems like I should be over this, or that it
shouldn't have happened in the first place.

And it's easy to feel angry with God, just like Jonah. But even in his anger we discover two things. First, we see that Jonah knew God's character all along, saying to God, "I knew that you are a gracious and compassionate God, slow to anger and abounding in love."

Second, we learn that God met Jonah in his anger and lovingly reminded Jonah of His love. When Jonah was frustrated that things didn't go the way he thought they should, God didn't punish him. Instead, God was patient and gently corrected Jonah so he could understand God's heart.

When we struggle, when we walk through hard things, it is natural to feel angry. Sometimes those feelings will be surprising. Maybe you are tired and feel as if God let you down. Maybe you feel angry that He allowed certain things to happen in your life. Maybe there isn't a word for how you feel toward God in the middle of your pain.

It's okay. Really.

The secret is to take it to the Lord. Don't hide it. Don't pretend it's not there. Take it to Him, and let Him meet you where you are.

We can know who God is, what His character is like, and still take our frustration to Him because He will meet us with graciousness and compassion. No matter what you feel toward God, take it to Him today and He will help you see His faithfulness.

LET'S PRAY

Lord, I have so many feelings about what is going on in me. Right now I feel _____ and _____. Show me Your grace and compassion in this place. Amen.

Will It Always Be This Way?

If any of you lacks wisdom, you should ask God,
who gives generously to all without finding fault,
and it will be given to you.

–James 1:5

Think about something you've been dealing with for a long time. I mean a really long time—something that goes back years or even decades. It could be a dream that feels lost or the pain from a situation or relationship you'd rather forget, or maybe it's something that goes as far back as your childhood. Whatever it is, pretend you're holding it in your hands.

How do you feel about holding this? How does your body feel? What do you notice?

The tender places in our hearts, the ones that go deep through time, are easy to ignore; we think we should be over these pains and struggles by now. But if we never really look at them, never really deal with them, they don't disappear. They just gather dust. And those dusty things we carry can seem like they will always be there, like nothing will ever change.

God wants more for us than carrying around dusty pain that feels endless. God wants freedom for us, even from the things that seem like they will never go away.

When we carry pain for a long time, we start wondering how long it will last. How long will we have to carry this heavy thing? How long will it hurt? After some time passes, those questions lead to a new question, one we hate to ask for fear that we already know the answer:

Will it always be this way? Will we always carry this, always feel the weight of it?

The pretty answer is that it will get better, and it might. But the real answer is that there are things we need to accept on our road to healing.

For example, the fact that my biological father left when I was three will not change. It will always be true; there is loss that goes with that fact. It's something I need to accept. Some of the things that go with that fact are emotional pain, difficulty in relationships, and trust issues. Those are the things I can heal and find freedom from.

Now think about the pain you're holding that's gathering dust. Look at it. Turn it over in your mind, and look at as many angles as you can see. What parts of that pain are facts that you have to accept, and what parts are things you can find healing from?

Maybe your best friend betrayed you. That is the fact you find acceptance for. The feelings that everyone will betray you, that you are always going to be alone, that there is something unlikeable about you—those are the places where you can discover healing.

There are so many possibilities here, but you know your own dusty pains that you have carried for so long. And the best part is, you don't need to figure this out on your own. God will give you the wisdom you need to move forward in healing, even from those things you've been carrying for years.

LET'S PUT IT INTO PRACTICE

Think about the things you've been carrying for years, and read today's verse from James as you seek God for wisdom and healing.

Don't Turn Back

Even in times of trouble we have a joyful confidence,
knowing that our pressures will develop in us patient
endurance. And patient endurance will refine our
character, and proven character
leads us back to hope.

–Romans 5:3–4, TPT

Reaching the top of another hill, I bent over, resting my hands on my knees, and tried to catch my breath. All I really wanted was for my heart rate to slow, my breathing to steady, and to be back in my nice air-conditioned car. I didn't think that was too much to ask.

My husband and I were hiking up Bluff Head. It's as intense as it sounds—at least for me. The view is gorgeous, but the climb is rough. Hills always do me in. I can walk on flat ground for miles without issue, but an incline always pushes me to my limits.

As I stood there, sweaty and tired, I wanted to turn around and head back to the car. But because of the route we took, turning around would actually take longer than finishing the loop we started. If I wanted the hike to end sooner, I had to keep climbing.

Our healing journey is like that. You may be fine one day and think everything is going great, but you suddenly reach a point when something triggers you. When we are put to the test like that, we can feel we are weak, as if we haven't made progress, and that everything is just too hard. It could be facing an issue you buried long ago: Maybe it is forgiving someone even though they never asked or even apologized, or navigating feelings of envy that arise when you wish you could get pregnant and your friend has a healthy baby, or watching someone else get your dream job.

Whatever it is, it triggers a wave of emotions and hurt—feelings that make you want to turn back and give up on this healing journey because it is so uncomfortable. Paul the apostle knew this feeling, and he encouraged us with the truth that our "patient endurance will refine our character, and proven character leads us back to hope."

You will face things that make you want to head for the safety of what is familiar and easy. But the truth is never found in that place. Hope is never found in that place. Even on my hike, turning back would have actually been harder than continuing. Your triggers are not there as a sign of your defeat. They are a sign that you are moving through a process. You are making progress in this journey. You are actively seeking the healing you long for.

You can manage these triggers when you hold on to the hope Paul reminds us of. Enduring through those moments may mean pushing on. It also may mean resting, practicing self-care, seeking help, and giving yourself a moment to catch your breath. But it never means turning back. You can endure today because of the hope you have in God's promises.

LET'S REFLECT

What things trigger you, making you want to turn back on your healing journey? What can you do the next time you feel that way?

You Can Do Hard Things

After this, Job lived a hundred and forty years;
he saw his children and their children to the
fourth generation. And so Job died,
an old man and full of years.

–Job 42:16–17

I haven't always liked the book of Job in the Bible. Am I allowed to say that? Maybe it's not exactly that I don't like it and rather that it scares me.

Job was known for being righteous, for living a good life that honored God. But Satan thought Job wasn't really doing it for the right reasons, so God allowed Satan to test Job. And this is where it scares me.

Job loses everything—not just some things, but literally everything. He loses his belongings, his livelihood, his family, his friends, and his health.

It's all gone, ripped away from him painfully and without an end in sight. Job even falters somewhat in his faith. But he brings it all to God. And God blesses him.

The ending is good. There are double blessings and Job has hope. That part doesn't scare me. It's all the loss, the pain, the heartache. Whenever I would hear anything about the book of Job, I wanted to stay as far away as I could for fear that I would have to face some of the same loss he did.

Even writing these words feels silly, but it's true. I don't want to catch what Job had because it feels too hard.

There are a few problems with this way of thinking, but the main one is that I'm focused on the wrong part. It isn't a question of whether we will have hard things in our lives. If you and I were sitting across from each other, we could share all the hard things we've been through and are going through. We all have loss, pain, worry, trauma—all of it. We're all walking through hard things in the world every day. The part that matters is what we will do when we face those hard things. Ultimately, will we hide from them, or will we take them to God?

There was nothing magical about Job that made him capable of enduring such heartache and struggle. The only thing that got him through it was choosing to do it with God. Over and over, each time it hurt, Job chose to go to God.

Sometimes his path to God was a bit longer. It's the same way with us. Job reminds us that we can do hard things. Our heartaches and pain do not define who we are. Our righteousness defines who we are.

I know righteousness is a big word that can feel awkward and maybe hard to live up to. But this righteousness doesn't come from anything we do. It comes straight from God, a gift for us as His children.

When we remember who we are and the gifts God gives us, we are reminded of what we are truly capable of. We are capable of faith no matter what circumstances we face. Job didn't get lost in his heartache, and we don't have to, either. We can do hard things because of who we are in Christ.

LET'S PRAY

Lord, You alone make me righteous, and who You are in me equips me to walk through hard things. Thank You for making me righteous in You. Amen.

Line in the Sand

Therefore, if anyone is in Christ, he is a new creation.
The old has passed away; behold, the new has come.

−2 Corinthians 5:17, ESV

Will you keep going? It's an important question and one we looked at recently. Choosing to persevere through the hard places of healing is something only you can decide to do. But there's a second question that is the real game changer.

Will you keep going the way you always have?

Naturally, you want to say no, of course not. You are walking forward in healing. You are changing. Things look and feel different. But moving into true freedom is more than just dealing with the issues you face.

I read a post online once that said you should end relationships with people who have hurt you or who impede your growth. Just end them—completely. The post insisted this was the key to moving forward. In some cases, that might be true. But it didn't sit right with me.

The idea of completely ending a relationship with someone I love just didn't feel right, even if the relationship or person was less than perfect. I prayed about it, thought about it, and thought and prayed some more.

There are situations where we should absolutely end a relationship. When we can't decide that for ourselves, the help of a professional counselor offers clarity on these issues to ensure our health and safety.

But what about when we want to keep people in our lives but still protect ourselves? How do we handle a relationship with a sibling, parent, spouse, or friend when there is both emotional pain and love? We need to draw a line in the sand.

Think about the behaviors that are healthy and safe for you in that relationship. How can you foster those, to interact in ways that don't cause more harm? How can you appreciate and love the other person while valuing the progress you're making toward healing?

The one-word answer for this is *boundaries*. There are great resources to help understand how this works in different relationships and settings, but the basic premise is valuing yourself enough to not allow hurtful, destructive behavior from the people in your life.

Maybe this looks like only visiting with a certain person in public settings. It could be that you limit your time with someone, or maybe you calmly end a phone conversation when that person is hurting you.

These are the lines in the sand: the lines that define what you allow and don't allow in those relationships. You'll need to think about them and decide ahead of time what lines you are not willing to allow anyone to cross anymore because doing so causes you harm.

Before you reflect more on what your boundaries are, say these words aloud to yourself: "I am worthy of being in safe and healthy relationships." Now say them again and maybe even a third time. Sometimes we need to hear truth over and over to believe it.

You can walk forward in your healing today by remembering that you can set boundaries because you are worthy of them. You are a new creation in Christ, worthy of love and respect and healing. Remember who you are, and draw your line in the sand.

LET'S PUT IT INTO PRACTICE

Choose one healthy boundary you can set that will help you maintain and move forward in your healing. Write it down.

It Isn't Fair

I have said these things to you, that in me you may
have peace. In the world you will have tribulation.
But take heart; I have overcome the world.

–John 16:33, ESV

I held the playing cards in my hand, carefully arranging sets that went together. I had my hearts all together and a great group of tens at the ready. My daughter had begged me to let her teach me how to play gin rummy. I kind of knew how to play, but there were details I didn't know, such as the scoring rules and how to win. I paid attention to her explanation and knew I was so close to winning. I just needed one or two more cards.

That's when she called, "Gin!" She was so excited as she spread her cards on the table for me to see. I was so close to winning, but she beat me. Not only that, but this was my fourth consecutive loss. I'm not a competitive person, but it just didn't seem fair.

Sometimes loss is like that. When we hold our loss up to compare it to someone else's loss, we think about how unfair it all is. How we deserved so much better. How we wish it were different.

The losses we face in life are much more significant than losing a game of cards. But somehow it's still easy to end up in the same place.

The loss of a pregnancy feels so unfair; we did everything right. The loss of a job is unjust; it should have been someone else. The loss of security isn't right; we all deserve to feel safe.

Whatever the loss is, it feels unjust. Like we've been robbed of something we deserve. More time, more love, more opportunity— whatever it is, we deserve more.

God knew we would feel that way. In John, Jesus's best friends were facing the most sorrow they would ever know. It hadn't even happened yet, and Jesus spoke absolute truth to them: "In the world you will have tribulation." He didn't deny the hardship they would feel, the loss and lament they would need to walk through. He recognized it. And then He did something so loving.

Jesus showed them the hope they have, even in their loss: "But take heart; I have overcome the world."

No matter what loss you are facing, Jesus sees it. God doesn't pretend your loss isn't there. He recognizes all that you will walk through, and He leaves you with the promise that He will overcome.

Loss may be uncomfortable, and it may not feel fair, but you can have hope that God will help you in that place. He will be present with you, and He will overcome the world. You can hold on to the same hope Jesus offered His disciples 2,000 years ago. It was for them, and it is for you.

LET'S PRAY

Father, sometimes things feel so unfair. Help me in the places I feel loss and heartache. Show me Your love, and remind me of the hope I have in You. Amen.

I'm Not the Same Person

Beloved, we are God's children right now; however, it is not yet apparent what we will become. But we do know that when it is finally made visible, we will be just like him, for we will see him as he truly is.

–1 John 3:2, TPT

The town fair is coming up next month in my hometown. It's a big deal, lasting three days, with a parade and rides and the tastiest food you could imagine. Living in an agricultural town, we'll have cows and horse pulls and baby chicks all on display just across from the big Ferris wheel and the balloon dart game.

Since I live in the town I grew up in, I know exactly what will happen at the fair. I will see people who knew me *when*: when my hair was permed and my skin was smooth, when my biggest worry was getting to class on time and whether a boy liked me, when I was a different person than I am today.

Maybe I was naïve or young or just less broken by life. Maybe I was more broken then, not understanding all the healing I really longed for. Maybe I was just different. I'm not exactly sure what to do with that today.

My first inclination is to stuff myself back into a mold of who I was. To show up looking as young and put together as I can, hoping that people will see the me that existed before I walked through some of the broken places, and definitely the me that fit into single digit–size jeans.

But I don't have to be who I was. Not the me I was in high school or my 20s or even yesterday. I don't have to be anyone other than who I am in this moment.

We are allowed to change. I know that seems obvious, but sometimes we hold ourselves to expectations to be both who we were before and who we hope to be tomorrow. In our minds, we expect our skin to be 16 and our wisdom to be 40. We expect our life to feel carefree and our house to show how grown up we are. We expect so much of ourselves. But we can't be everything all at once. We need to give ourselves permission to be who we are today.

Today you are a woman who is pursuing healing. You are a woman who is strong and faithful in her journey, even when it doesn't look perfect; a woman who is growing in her faith in a thousand tiny steps instead of leaps and bounds; a woman who is in process. Just as John reminds us, "it is not yet apparent what we will become."

You don't have to be who you were. And you are not yet who you will be. Today you have permission to be exactly you. The you that exists in the process of healing, in the middle of brokenness, without being tied to yesterday or running for tomorrow.

You are not the same as you were. And that is a good thing.

LET'S REFLECT

How have you changed since your teens? How do you feel about where you are today? What does the phrase "in process" mean for you?

Can I Really Do This?

Do not conform to the pattern of this world, but be transformed by the renewing of your mind. Then you will be able to test and approve what God's will is—his good, pleasing and perfect will.

—Romans 12:2

It's easy to think that the followers of Jesus had it all together. After all, these disciples, the apostles, the friends of Jesus, walked with Him. They learned from Him. They actually lived in the same time period. Many of these people also wrote the books of the New Testament. And many of them struggled just like us.

Paul is one of the great examples of this. Much like us, he didn't actually meet Jesus in the flesh. His experience was with the resurrected Jesus, and it was life changing.

He wasn't even named Paul for the first part of his life; rather, his name was Saul. He hated the people who followed Jesus. He even had them persecuted and killed. But then something changed. When Saul encountered Jesus, he became a new person.

Instead of persecuting people, he welcomed them. Instead of stoning people, he taught them truth and showed them love. He walked through his own healing journey, and it blesses us today.

Paul went from angry and broken to walking in peace and faith. It wasn't something he could do on his own. It came from the mercy of God. His experience not only helped him, but it shows us how to go from our broken places to freedom.

Lucky for us, Paul has a lot of wisdom to share about going from hard, broken places to living your life in healing newness. That's why we can trust what he writes. It's as if he is writing to himself as much as he is writing to us.

In Romans, Paul writes about Israel and shares how Jesus's mercy changes everything. Paul knows what that mercy is like. And it's not just about a change in circumstances: Right after he shares about Israel, Paul addresses the importance of what happens in our minds.

When Paul said, "Be transformed by the renewing of your mind," he knew that we would need the reminder to allow the transformation brought by God into all aspects of our lives, even our minds.

When we walk our healing journey, it's easy to focus on the heart and dismiss the mind. But when we do that, we leave a gap, an open place where doubt and negative thoughts can sneak in and threaten our progress.

Negative thoughts are normal. They're part of our journey to build our faith in God as we walk through our healing. But we don't have to welcome them in and make them a place to stay. We are transformed in the renewing of our minds by Jesus.

Transformation and renewal don't come through our own strength but through the mercy and love of God. Let's walk in that transformation today!

LET'S PRAY

Father, thank You for Your mercy and the way You change my heart. I trust You to go deeper than that, to transform my mind that I may experience full healing in You. Amen.

Remove the Barriers

Get rid of all bitterness, rage and anger, brawling and slander, along with every form of malice.

–Ephesians 4:31

Wouldn't it be nice if our journey toward healing was smooth; if it was like walking down a nice paved path with a beautiful view and signs always pointing us in the right direction? If there were no crossroads that left us wondering which way to go or potholes that left us feeling a bit battered?

Raise your hand if your journey has been smooth. (If we were in a room together, everyone would be looking around to see if someone raised their hand. Let me tell you, no one would. Not one person.)

Our journeys are never perfect. It seems there are always barriers that rise up, seemingly out of nowhere. Maybe it's the unexpected person you run into or a fresh wound that is inflicted; maybe it's a memory or a delay; or, maybe it's something inside you, something you're holding on to.

One of the most common barriers to our own healing is ourselves. We hold on to things from the past and carry them with us. We look at other people's journeys and think about how ours should be like theirs. We smile and keep going even though we are still angry, bitter, or resentful.

Every one of these things is like a barrier we erect on our path. We can't blame other people for these things; we do them all on our own. We are responsible for these obstacles, and knowing that makes it even worse.

This isn't the perfect, pretty part of healing. This is the part when we get our hands dirty and go deep. This is when we look at what we are doing and ask God to help us get out of our own way.

The best thing we can do for ourselves is identify and remove the barriers to our healing as much as we are able. One of the sneakiest barriers we erect is resentment. It often comes from an injury that leads us to have negative emotional reactions. Unlike anger, resentment stays long after the injustice we faced has faded. We hold on to it, sometimes for years, leaving it to simmer in the background of everything we do.

Resentment keeps us tied to the wound instead of free to seek healing. That simmering anger or distrust holds us back, blocking our way toward the thing we really want the most. And here's the really insidious part: It usually feels justified.

Distrust toward men after a man has hurt you? It feels justified. Fear of driving after a bad accident? It feels justified. Anger toward the person responsible for your job loss? It feels justified. This list could fill pages. But these examples are all the same. They stem from a negative emotion that keeps you tied to the past.

You are here because you want freedom and healing. You've lived in the feelings of the past for long enough. Today you can choose to untie yourself from those negative feelings and remove those barriers in your path so you can walk forward.

Of course, there will be barriers that come up that are not your doing, things that are out of your control. God will show you how to handle those. But today, remove as many barriers from your path as you can.

LET'S PUT IT INTO PRACTICE

List the barriers you place in your own way. Ask God to help you remove them so you can walk in healing!

I Don't Deserve This

But I tell you, do not resist an evil person. If anyone
slaps you on the right cheek, turn to them the other
cheek also. And if anyone wants to sue you and take
your shirt, hand over your coat as well. If anyone
forces you to go one mile, go with them two miles.
Give to the one who asks you, and do not turn away
from the one who wants to borrow from you.

–Matthew 5:39–42

Matthew 5 is one of the most beautiful passages of Jesus's teaching. It
is often known for the beginning section, and people love to quote the
gentle poetry of what is known as the Beatitudes.

"Blessed are the poor in spirit, for theirs is the kingdom of heaven"
(Matthew 5:3) is how Jesus begins. And those of us who feel a bit down,
a bit poor in spirit, we like that blessing and promise.

Jesus continues with blessings and promises for those who mourn
(Matthew 5:4) and the meek (Matthew 5:5) and the pure in heart (Matthew 5:8). Blessings and promises are soothing to our worn and weary
souls. Jesus knew we would need to start with those things before we
could be ready for the rest of His teaching.

The rest of Matthew 5 goes deep and doesn't skirt the hard issues.
Adultery, murder, the law, relationships—Jesus talks about it all.
Although He always teaches in love, these are hard topics.

Perhaps one of the hardest is forgiveness. In the part of the chapter
quoted here, we encounter the teaching that doesn't make sense to our
logical minds. It also happens to be an often-abused and misused section of scripture: "If anyone slaps you on the right cheek, turn to them
the other cheek also."

Many people have used this to justify unhealthy, dangerous behavior. Jesus has never been about putting us in danger. So let's look at what He is truly saying here.

In a world defined by law and what should be just and fair, Jesus turns everything upside down. He challenges the law and what feels logical. It feels logical that when one is harmed, she should not be harmed again. And maybe she even has a right to fight back. That's the logic of the world.

But Jesus reminds us that logic isn't faith. Logic isn't love. When we are tempted to think, *I don't deserve this*, or, *I should get even*, Jesus reminds us what love looks like. He's setting the stage for the ultimate demonstration of love on the cross.

Let's be clear: Jesus's teaching absolutely does not justify abuse. It does not condone or encourage victimhood. That is not who Jesus is.

Instead, Jesus encourages us to look beyond the offense to offer love. He longs for us to love others the way He loves: full of grace and mercy. Although it may not seem fair, Jesus calls us all to respond with forgiveness and love.

Maybe you feel you don't deserve the wrong that was done to you, or maybe you feel justified in your anger. Instead of holding on to that, you can respond with the forgiveness and love Jesus tells us about, always remembering the blessings and promises He offers to you along the way.

LET'S REFLECT

Do you ever feel like you don't deserve the hurt you are walking through? Jesus agrees. And that is why He offers blessings for you first. How can you embrace His blessings and His teachings to offer love and forgiveness?

We Are Called to Forgive

Very rarely will anyone die for a righteous person,
though for a good person someone might possibly
dare to die. But God demonstrates his own love for us
in this: While we were still sinners, Christ died for us.

–*Romans 5:7–8*

My biological father has never apologized for leaving me. That's a hard sentence to write, mostly because I want it to be different. Not because I'm seeking a relationship with him, but because it feels wrong. When someone hurts you, they should apologize. That's how I feel.

But *should* is a tricky word. It is based on a sense of right and wrong, a picture in our heads, and a handful of other factors such as upbringing and social experiences and norms. The bottom line is that *should* is undependable.

I like to think of *should* as a colander. It's the thing we hold on to, and life is what we pour in. Some things stay in the colander. But some things go right through the holes, leaving us unable to hold on to them, no matter how hard we try.

If that colander of *should* is so unreliable, why do we keep holding it? And why do we run everything through it?

Jesus didn't. As a matter of fact, Jesus poured his whole self right out. "You see, at just the right time, when we were still powerless, Christ died for the ungodly" (Romans 5:6).

Jesus gave His whole life for people who might not have even liked Him—gave it for others when it didn't make sense. It would make sense to say He died for those who loved Him. He died for His disciples, or He died for Peter, James, and John—the ones He was closest to—or even for Mary and Martha and Lazarus because they were so dear to Him.

But Jesus died for those who didn't know Him, who didn't even want to know Him.

That's how forgiveness can feel: undeserved, unearned, unwarranted. But all of those *uns* are not enough to cancel out the need for forgiveness. We are called to forgive others not because it is earned but because it is needed.

The person who hurt you years ago and never asked for your forgiveness needs it. The partner who betrayed you and crushed your dreams needs your forgiveness. The friend who left and never looked back needs your forgiveness. My biological father, who never asked for it, needs my forgiveness.

Forgiveness is a necessary part of healing, especially when it doesn't feel earned. You get to choose whom to forgive and when. But the sooner you do it, the sooner you can experience freedom.

You should know, it won't be easy. It might take time. But you can do hard things, and you have a Savior walking with you for all of your days. You may not feel like people in your life deserve forgiveness, but you can offer it just the same. You don't even have to tell them. Just start with forgiving them in your heart, and see where God leads you.

LET'S PRAY

God, forgiveness seems so hard. I don't even think they deserve it. But I know You offer it just the same. Help me forgive the way You forgive, fully and completely, so I can move forward in freedom. Amen.

Joy Is Part of Your Healing

"This day is holy to God, your God. Don't weep and carry on [. . .] Go home and prepare a feast, holiday food and drink; and share it with those who don't have anything: This day is holy to God. Don't feel bad. The joy of God is your strength!"

–Nehemiah 8:9–10, MSG

Right now you're in the middle of hard work. It may not be the sweaty, dirt-under-your-fingernails type of hard work, but that doesn't make it any easier. Seeking emotional healing is difficult and requires a lot from you.

Nehemiah knew a bit about hard work—and heart work. Back in the Old Testament, Zerubbabel and Ezra both tried to fix the ruined state of Jerusalem, but they failed. Enter Nehemiah. The thing he is most known for is building a wall around the city. He worked hard to restore the city by doing the difficult task of rebuilding. Naturally, he faced opposition. Not everyone was on the same page.

It can feel that way with the work we do in our hearts, too. Here we are, digging in and doing the hard work, only to face challenges and opposition. But we can learn from Nehemiah.

He kept doing the work. He pressed on through the opposition, through the challenges, through the naysayers, Nehemiah pressed on in what God told him to do because he had hope for the restoration promised by the prophets who came before him.

We have those same promises. And we have that hope. This is what makes the amazing happen.

Nehemiah and Ezra experienced restoration. They began to see the fruit of their hard work. They even chose to celebrate it, calling people to "Go home and prepare a feast, holiday food and drink; and share it with those who don't have anything: This day is holy to God." They celebrated while the restoration was still happening. It wasn't complete. It was in process, like us.

Then Nehemiah went a step further, reminding people, "Don't feel bad. The joy of God is your strength!" Nehemiah sought joy as part of the healing process for the people.

God wants us to seek joy in our process, too. Joy is part of the healing.

Unfortunately, Nehemiah didn't stay in that place, and neither did the people. They began to shift their focus back to the past, to their pain. Instead of looking ahead with hope in the promises of the prophets, they reverted to the old ways of thinking and living. Joy in the Lord was no longer part of their process.

The problem that arose for Nehemiah and the people was that they didn't continue to hold room for joy and hope. The core issues in their hearts were never fixed because they needed the transformation that could only come with making space for joy and hope as they changed.

Now you're here doing the work. And you get to decide. Will you make room for joy and hope in your healing? Will you make space for the joy of the Lord to transform your heart so you can walk forward in His promises?

The joy of the Lord truly is your strength in healing. Walk forward believing it today.

LET'S PUT IT INTO PRACTICE

Write down three ways you can find joy in the process of your healing, and put them into practice today.

Hope Always Shines Again

The Lord makes firm the steps of the one who delights in him; though he may stumble, he will not fall, for the Lord upholds him with his hand.

–Psalm 37:23–24

The idea of choosing joy looks great on paper. It even makes a great T-shirt. But what do you do when it's not that easy—when choosing joy feels completely impossible?

That road is a direct route to feeling hopeless.

It doesn't matter the circumstances that get you there, hopelessness has a way of consuming everything—even the things you know are good, like choosing joy in your healing. Hopelessness can be like a fog that covers everything you see.

But there is something to remember about fog: It always lifts.

Imagine driving on a long road. You pack a cooler with snacks and throw your beach chair in the back of the car, along with the book you've been saving just for today. The beginning of the drive is smooth, with great music on the radio and an iced latte in the cup holder. But as you get closer to the beach, you notice it's a little harder to see. You begin to wonder if it's a good day for the beach, but you have waited too long for this opportunity. You drive on.

Soon the fog that was gently saying hello is now making you turn down the music so you can concentrate. You know the road is there, but you can't see much past your front bumper. Your driving slows, and you wonder if you're still going the right way.

After a few slow miles, you pull over just to make sure you're on the right path. The GPS says the beach is just a mile ahead, but you can't see anything that remotely resembles the beach town you know. You have a choice. Do you keep going, trusting that the beach is there and the fog will lift, or do you head back?

The choice is always yours.

Hopelessness is that fog. It covers everything, hiding what you know to be true, making you doubt the maps and guides that promise you'll get there. But the fog of hopelessness doesn't ever change what's really there. Remember, "The Lord makes firm the steps of the one who delights in him." You can trust that God will make your way firm, even in the fog.

Sometimes you may have to pause and give yourself a little time to let it lift. Maybe you need to ask for help to see through the fog, to get where you're going. Maybe you slow down but drive on. No matter what, the fog will eventually lift.

In your healing, you may experience moments of hopelessness. It may cover everything like a dense fog, making you doubt where you're going or how far you've come. But the beach is still there, friend. Even in the fog, the beach is there.

LET'S REFLECT

Have you ever experienced feeling hopeless? Are you feeling that right now in your healing journey? How can you rest, look for help, or press on through that feeling?

When You Don't Ask

Carry each other's burdens, and in this way you will
fulfill the law of Christ.

—Galatians 6:2

My sister-in-law and I sat in my favorite coffee shop. I don't even
drink coffee, but I love the small spot tucked into the corner of the
town green. We were at the little window table, and I'm sure I had a
cookie because cookies make most things better. We were having a
hard conversation.

"You never need help," she said to me.

I was about to start talking, but she continued: "I know you *need*
help, but you always act like you don't. And that makes it hard for me to
get close to you."

The very thing I wanted, to have a closer relationship, was the thing
she felt I was preventing. Part of me wanted to deny it. I wanted to
explain how it wasn't true, that I needed people, that I asked for help.
But I knew she was right.

In my quest to keep it all together, to always show up for other
people, to brush my struggles under the rug, to do it all, I didn't let
others see the weakness in me. I could try to make excuses, but I knew
it was really because I was afraid.

Asking for help meant admitting my weak places. It meant admitting that I didn't have it all under control. If people saw my weakness,
my need, I was afraid of two things.

First, I thought it meant I had failed. If I needed help, it was an
admission that I couldn't handle all the things that life threw my way.
It also meant that I was admitting I wasn't perfect. Second, I was afraid
that people wouldn't step up—that they would see my weakness and it
would be too much for them. They would walk away.

I looked right across that table and said two words: "You're right." It would have been easier to deny it and say she was wrong and that, of course, I needed people. But I chose to be vulnerable.

Asking for help sounds like a good idea, until we realize the first step is an admission that we need help, followed closely by the choice to be vulnerable with another person. We all have different experiences that make this process unique to us, but the basics are still there, and it can feel scary.

But it can also feel freeing.

I would love to tell you that when you admit you need help and step out and ask for it, you will always get what you need; that people will always know and understand, hold your hand, and support you in just the right way. Truthfully, that's not likely. But it is certain that if you never ask, no one will ever know how to help.

Basically, it's never going to be a 100 percent sure thing. But isn't 75 percent better than zero? When we never ask for help, we are standing firm on that zero. But when we take the risk and admit we need help, then ask for it, we see that number creeping higher and higher as we walk forward in healing.

It's all about finding a person you feel comfortable reaching out to. It could be a family member or a friend. Maybe it's a trusted member of your church or community. If you are unsure or need someone outside your circles, a therapist or counselor is a trusted person to ask for help who won't judge you or your circumstances. Professional help is not a last resort, and there is never shame in seeking it. All of these options are resources you can use—when you ask.

God is always faithful to help us, and sometimes He does it through the people in our lives.

LET'S PUT IT INTO PRACTICE

Think of one way you can ask someone for help today and do it—big or small, just ask!

Pick Up Your Mat

When Jesus saw him lying there and learned that he had been in this condition for a long time, he asked him, "Do you want to get well?"

–John 5:6

In the book of John, we see so much of what Jesus can do. By John 5, we are already well on our way to seeing that He can perform miracles. He has followers and has chatted with the Samaritan woman and turned water into wine. It's clear Jesus is a big deal.

At the beginning of the chapter, Jesus heads to Jerusalem for a festival. That's when He walked by the spot where many disabled people would lie. There was a pool that people believed made them well. Many others avoided the area or ignored the disabled people—but not Jesus. That's precisely the path Jesus decided to take. That's when Jesus encountered the man.

We don't know his name, but this man had been suffering for almost 40 years. That's a long time to be in pain and to be so close to where people go for healing. Imagine being so close to your healing but feeling unable to get there.

Of course, Jesus talked to the man. I can picture Jesus looking right into his eyes, asking the question, "Do you want to get well?" Was it an accusation? Jesus is too loving for that. It was a heart question.

Immediately, the man gave reasons why he couldn't get to this healing pool. The man didn't know Jesus could offer what he longed for. He laid his desperation out for Jesus instead of answering the question. And still Jesus offered grace.

"Then Jesus said to him, 'Get up! Pick up your mat and walk.' At once the man was cured; he picked up his mat and walked" (John 5:8–9).

There was no back-and-forth. There was no asking again. Jesus simply gave the man what He knew was needed. He saw the man's heart and gave the healing he longed for. It's beautiful.

But there's one part we can miss if we skip right to the man walking for the first time in nearly four decades. There's an order of events, and it matters.

1. As soon as Jesus said it, the man was cured—right away, no delay.

2. The man picked up his mat.

3. The man walked.

The most overlooked step is the middle one: picking up the mat. When Jesus brings healing, we have a responsibility if we want to walk in that healing. We have to pick up the mat.

The man was cured, but he couldn't walk away until he got up off the mat he had been lying on. Imagine how scary it was for that man. He hadn't walked in 38 years. And now he was just going to believe this stranger had healed him? He was going to stand up on legs that had never worked—while everyone was watching?

What if Jesus is offering us healing, but we're just too afraid to get up? What if we are so worried about what it will look like or what people will think that we don't stand? When we are seeking healing, we have to stand before we can walk.

LET'S REFLECT

Imagine Jesus asking you, "Do you want to get well?" What would you say? How is Jesus calling you to stand up and walk in your healing today?

You're Already Free

At last we have freedom, for Christ has set us free! We must always cherish this truth and firmly refuse to go back into the bondage of our past.

–Galatians 5:1, TPT

On our way home from dinner recently, my husband and I had an argument. We were talking about plans for the weekend. He wanted to go somewhere, and I didn't think it was a good idea. We went back and forth as we drove home from dinner, giving our best arguments to prove we were right.

"But we have the time, and it would be so great, and I don't understand what the big deal is."

"I know, but what about all the other things we need to do, and you didn't even think about the money."

Round and round we went for the two-mile car ride. Please tell me silly arguments like this happen to you, too. Looking back, I know it was not worth the energy I put into it. It was a little thing that we could work out together. And we did. But something familiar was triggered inside me when we were arguing.

I heard that little internal voice saying that he would leave. That this would be the thing that made him run for the hills.

This argument lasted three minutes, and here I was listening to this inner voice, rooted in fears from the past. Fears that I had worked on, trying to break the hold they had on me. Fears that always tried to turn my focus back to bondage instead of the freedom God gives me.

The past has a way of doing that. It would be great if we could banish the fears and pains of the past and they never bothered us again. But sometimes they creep in. They make another try at turning us around to lock the shackles on our hearts.

You've come far enough in your healing journey to know that your freedom comes in Christ, and to know that you are no longer tied to your past hurt. You are free.

It's easy, reflexive almost, to turn back. As hard as that place of bondage was, at least you know what to expect. It's the worst kind of comfortable. But you don't live there anymore.

Moving forward in freedom requires things of you: faith, courage, resolve. They are big things that take you to unfamiliar places. But that is exactly what Jesus wants for you. To walk in freedom means to have faith, to be courageous, and to keep your eyes forward with resolve.

Don't go back to your former bondage. Keep walking forward in the freedom Christ has already given you.

LET'S PRAY

Lord, help me keep my eyes focused on You and the freedom You've given me. When I am tempted to turn back to the bondage You have freed me from, give me the faith, courage, and resolve to stand firm in You. Amen.

Dress the Part

"Truly I tell you, if you have faith as small as a mustard seed, you can say to this mountain, 'Move from here to there,' and it will move. Nothing will be impossible for you."

—*Matthew 17:20*

I woke up on a rainy day just wanting to stay in bed. It was the perfect day to pull the covers up and watch a movie instead of getting up to do the things that really needed to get done. But they were things that had to happen.

Getting up, I took a shower and stood in front of my closet in my robe. My rainy-day mood was pulling me to cozy sweats. I could just wear them and be comfortable all day, a compromise between getting up and staying in bed. But I knew those cozy sweats wouldn't help me shift from rainy-day mode to getting things done. As much as I wanted to wear them, they would only keep me longing for a lazy day and my warm bed.

So I grabbed an easy, comfortable dress. Then I did something even more drastic: I put some makeup on and dried my hair. It wasn't anything elaborate, but I dressed for the day I needed to have. My clothes were the first step in taking me from lazy day to getting things done.

Sometimes healing is like that. We need to dress the part before we actually feel like dressing the part. Putting on a dress didn't do anything magical. But it did motivate me to keep going when I didn't feel like it. This isn't to say we never take a rest or stay in bed with our cozy sweats on. But we do need to be mindful and choose wisely.

If you want progress, there will be days you need to dress for it even though you don't want to. There will be days you need to face challenges, to seek God, and to read this devotional, even though you'd rather just get back in bed. Why is it important to keep going? Because you want, and are capable of, change.

When this feels heavy and too hard, when the world tells you you'll never get there, or when you can't seem to see the finish line, reflect on how far you have already come and know that God is by your side as you follow the path of healing.

God never said this process would be easy. And it does require something of you: faith. The good news is that you don't need huge faith. Remember, Jesus tells us we only need faith the size of a mustard seed to move a whole mountain. You only need the tiniest bit, a speck of faith, and God can use it for big things—even things that feel impossible.

There will be days on this journey when you feel like pulling the covers up and pretending the world doesn't exist. And sometimes that is exactly what you need to do. But sometimes you need to summon that seed of faith and choose to put your dress on when you don't feel like it. You need to make that tiny choice to shift from checking out to being intentional about staying present in this process. Then see what God does.

LET'S PUT IT INTO PRACTICE

Choose one way you can "dress the part" and summon that tiny seed of faith today.

Do I Have What It Takes?

Moses answered the people, "Do not be afraid.
Stand firm and you will see the deliverance the
Lord will bring you today. The Egyptians you see
today you will never see again. The Lord will
fight for you; you need only to be still."

–Exodus 14:13–14

I think we can all agree that Moses is pretty highly regarded when it comes to Bible characters. He witnessed great miracles, led thousands of people, and had divine, personal encounters with God. Sometimes I wonder if he was a biblical superhero.

But did you know he didn't embrace all of this easily? In fact, he doubted whether he was cut out to do what God called him to. And he doubted that more than once.

First, Moses was a shepherd. He led sheep, not people. When God called him to lead hundreds of thousands of humans, if not more, his response was, "Who am I that I should go to Pharaoh and bring the Israelites out of Egypt?" (Exodus 3:11). Moses didn't think he was good enough, even though God called him to do it.

Then he tried to explain to God how he didn't know enough: "Moses said to God, 'Suppose I go to the Israelites and say to them, "The God of your fathers has sent me to you," and they ask me, "What is his name?" Then what shall I tell them?'" (Exodus 3:13). But God wasn't having it, because God's plan was never about what Moses knew on his own.

Next, Moses was worried about whether people would even listen to or believe him. "Moses objected, 'They won't trust me. They won't listen to a word I say. They're going to say, "God? Appear to him? Hardly!"'" (Exodus 4:1, MSG).

That argument led right into how Moses didn't think he'd be a good speaker: "Moses raised another objection to God: 'Master, please, I don't talk well. I've never been good with words, neither before nor after you spoke to me. I stutter and stammer'" (Exodus 4:10, MSG).

Finally, he circled back to how he wasn't good enough to begin with and asked God to send someone else (Exodus 4:13).

Moses was full of doubt: doubt in who he was, doubt in his abilities, doubt in what God was calling him to. It all stemmed from lack of belief. His heart didn't believe he would be able to do what God said he would.

I'm beginning to think of Moses as less of a superhero and more of a friend I could have coffee with because I can relate to how he felt. Even in this journey, I wonder if I have what it takes to heal.

Do you have doubts, too? Could you pull up a chair with Moses and chat with him about feeling like you don't have what it takes?

Before we get too far, though, we get to hear the rest of Moses's story, and we are reminded: When you're doing anything with God, limitations, fears, and even your perceived failures are nothing compared to who God is and what He says you can do.

Look at today's verses again. Moses is transformed by God into a man full of confidence, able to lead his people, no longer troubled by any doubts, certain God will give them everything they need. Just as Moses realized, God promises to give you everything you need for this journey. If it is for His glory, He will equip you. And God is always in the process of making you healed and whole for eternity. Will you believe it?

LET'S REFLECT

Think about Moses's doubts. Can you relate to how he felt? Do you believe God will overcome those doubts you have about yourself and let you walk in freedom and healing?

Let's Talk about Sin

But because of his great love for us, God, who is rich
in mercy, made us alive with Christ even when we
were dead in transgressions—it is by grace you have
been saved [. . .] that in the coming ages he might
show the incomparable riches of his grace, expressed
in his kindness to us in Christ Jesus.

—Ephesians 2:4–5, 7

One of my least favorite topics is sin. In fact, I don't know anyone who likes to talk about sin—at least, not their own. We are quick to point out the sin in the people around us, the way my husband was short tempered with the kids or how that one friend is always gossiping. Talking about other people's sin feels safe because when we shine the spotlight on them, we can keep our own sin in the shadows.

So much of our emotional healing is based on other people's sin. It's easy to feel justified in pointing it out, giving ourselves the victim label and absolving ourselves of any responsibility in what happened or how we handled it. But God warns us about looking at everyone else's sin instead of our own.

When Jesus is teaching the people in Matthew, he hits on a lot of hard subjects, sin included: "Why would you focus on the flaw in someone else's life and fail to notice the glaring flaws of your own? How could you say to your friend, 'Let me show you where you're wrong,' when you're guilty of even more? You're being hypercritical and a hypocrite! First acknowledge and deal with your own 'blind spots,' and then you'll be capable of dealing with the 'blind spot' of your friend" (Matthew 7:3–5, TPT).

As Jesus says, it's a lot more comfortable to point out the sin we see in others than to look at our own, especially when it is connected to a tender emotional place in our hearts. But if we want healing, we need to look at the whole picture. And that means addressing our sin.

I don't know what emotional things you are seeking to heal. There is a very good chance that a lot of what you walked through is not your fault—at all. God sees that and knows that. This is in no way a condemnation of who you are or what you went through.

But with the most tender love and mercy, God invites us to open up fully and stop looking at the things that were done to us. Instead, we should look at ourselves and the ways we cope that are less than God's best for us; we should think about the responses we have in hard situations and admit our unbelief in God's love for us or the healing He has for us.

Looking at your own sin is another way to walk forward in greater healing and freedom. It may not feel comfortable, but God is with you every step of the way. It's why He died for you—so that right now, in this moment, you can find deeper healing and greater freedom.

LET'S PRAY

Lord, help me see the places where I have sinned and take them to You, fully confident that You will meet me with grace and kindness as You forgive me. Amen.

Lift Your Arms

When Moses' hands grew tired, they took a stone and put it under him and he sat on it. Aaron and Hur held his hands up—one on one side, one on the other—so that his hands remained steady till sunset.

–Exodus 17:12

It's easy to get tired in this process. Emotional healing isn't something we do passively. It's not something that we can hire out and just pay the bill at the end. It's something in which we are active. And even though we have hope in this place, it's okay to admit that it's a lot.

Moses knew that feeling. Even as he led the people from a place of bondage to a place of freedom and hope, he experienced hardship, heartache, and hard work. How does that help us? Well, it makes us feel a bit better.

In our journey to healing, we can link arms with one another and with the greats like Moses, and learn how to keep going. One of my favorite things Moses did actually came in a moment when he felt really tired.

The Israelites that he was leading were under attack. There was a battle going on. And Moses knew his goal was to remain faithful to God, just as we're trying to do.

Moses did something bold to show his focus. He stood on top of the hill during the battle and held up his hands and the staff of God. It was as if he were declaring victory before the battle was even over. It was a faith move. It was beautiful.

But we can't forget Moses was a real person, just like you and me. Have you ever held something up for a long time, or even just raised your hand for more than a few minutes? I have. And I discovered that your arm gets tired—fast. Guess what happened to Moses? His arms got tired.

He knew he was supposed to keep them raised to God throughout the battle, but his physical body was weary. This is when I often give up—when things get too hard, or I get too tired. But we can be like Moses when that happens. Instead of letting the struggle take our focus, we can keep turning to and trusting in God.

For Moses, that meant a place to sit and some trusted friends to hold up his arms when he needed a break. It was a place for his body to rest and some people to take the pressure off while still holding up those arms.

If you're tired, you can keep going. And you don't need to do it alone.

Ask God to help by giving you a break when you need it and sending people to take the pressure off for a bit. You can keep your eyes focused and your arms raised. Just ask God. He is ready to help you lift your arms high in victory today.

LET'S REFLECT

Are your arms raised in victory even though the process isn't over? Are you feeling tired? How can you find rest and support in that place today?

Stop Looking Around

The Lord will fulfill his purpose for me; your
steadfast love, O Lord, endures forever.
Do not forsake the work of your hands.

–Psalm 138:8, ESV

You don't want to take me to a restaurant. I am certain we'd have a great time sitting across the table and chatting. But when it comes to the food, well, you may need to watch your plate.

I'm famous for doing this with my husband. We'll go out to eat, and I'll hem and haw over the menu. He reads it quickly and makes a decision, but I'm caught in a battle between whether to order the things I really want or the healthy choices. Usually healthy wins. And you'd think that would be good.

Then the food comes. I look at mine, and it's lovely. It's exactly what I ordered. I should be thrilled. But then I look at my husband's food, and all I want is what he has. He ordered based on exactly what he felt like eating. It looks delicious.

Because he's so gracious, and we've been married so long, he always offers me some of his food. It makes me happier, and he knows that's better for both of us. Truthfully, if I had my healthy entrée all by myself, I would be fine. It's not until I see my choice sitting across from someone else's that I find myself comparing.

Most days on this healing path I'm content to do things at my own speed, in my own way, with God. It's just the right pace for me, and God is so faithful to walk with me in grace. But every once in a while I look to my left or right and see how someone else is doing it.

I watch how she is moving forward in healing much faster than I am, or, how another woman is doing it all with a smile on her face and a perfect manicure. I also see how another woman is healing multiple things at once instead of one tiny thing at a time.

The problem isn't how they're doing it. The problem isn't even how I'm doing it. The problem is when I look at how others are doing it and compare them to me. It all goes downhill when I compare my progress or speed or need for rest to someone else, thinking she's doing it better than I am.

The problem comes when you want what someone else has. There will always be other people walking through their healing differently. These people seem to have it figured out, while you can't make sense of what's happening; these people go faster or are more intentional or look prettier while doing it. These people are not you.

You're not supposed to be them, and your path isn't supposed to look like theirs. When you stop looking around and keep your eyes on Jesus, you will see the grace, mercy, and love you are walking in. You will see the progress and timing and hope God has for you right where you are. You will see your path to healing and love every step with Jesus.

LET'S PUT IT INTO PRACTICE

Write down three good things about where you are on your healing journey.

Is This Working?

But the fruit of the Spirit is love, joy, peace,
forbearance, kindness, goodness, faithfulness,
gentleness and self-control. Against such things
there is no law [. . .] Since we live by the Spirit,
let us keep in step with the Spirit.

—Galatians 5:22–23, 25

Paul wanted people to fully understand the freedom they have in Christ. Throughout the New Testament, we find him teaching, writing letters, and guiding others to understand exactly what being a believer means.

That tells me people were having a hard time understanding. That also makes me feel better because I have a hard time understanding, too.

When we are living in freedom, Paul tells us exactly what we find: things like love, joy, and gentleness. Those things are the fruits, the by-products, of living a life in freedom with Jesus. But they're not the only kinds of fruit.

I have fruit trees in my yard. They aren't anything fancy, but we have a few trees because my husband loves it. This year the fruit is looking healthy and plentiful. But it's not always that way. Sometimes the fruit can have disease, rot, or insects. Sometimes there's a complete lack of fruit. The very same trees can produce wildly different things depending on a lot of factors.

It's the same with us. Although we want to think we're strong, healthy trees always bearing the good things like peace and kindness and faithfulness, sometimes our fruit is less appealing.

Just before today's verse in Galatians, Paul talks about the fruit of living in the flesh. Things like jealousy, discord, and idolatry make the list (among others). As much as we'd like to claim we are always growing the fruit of the Spirit, we are here in the world, growing fruit of the flesh, too. Until the day we are in heaven with God, we will see fruits we don't like. It is part of our humanity. But the harvest tells a great deal about the state of our heart.

As you work on your emotional healing, you may wonder if you are getting anywhere. It can be hard to see if you're making progress when you're in the middle of things. The best thing to do is to look for the fruit.

Do you feel more peace than you did two months ago? Are you consumed with rage, or have you found new ways to be kind? Can you see flickers of joy in places that were once filled with sorrow? How does the fruit of your life look today?

Love. Joy. Peace. Forbearance. Kindness. Goodness. Faithfulness. Gentleness. Self-control. These are all the good fruits the Spirit of God grows in you.

Your emotional healing is directly connected to living in the freedom you have in Christ. When you feel like you're not making progress, when you're not sure you're better off today than you were a week ago, start to look for the evidence of good fruit in your life.

LET'S PRAY

Spirit of God, as I walk in healing, help me see the good fruits You are growing in my life. Show me love, joy, peace, forbearance, kindness, goodness, faithfulness, gentleness, and self-control as they grow more in me each day. Amen.

Extravagant Forgiveness

> Then Peter came to him and asked, "Lord, how often
> should I forgive someone who sins against me?
> Seven times?" "No, not seven times," Jesus
> replied, "but seventy times seven!"
>
> *–Matthew 18:21–22, NLT*

The last time I spoke to my father, I was pregnant with my first baby. It was a few weeks after Christmas, and my belly was stretched taut, all the excitement and fears of motherhood swirling inside me. We did our dance of apology and pretending. He apologized for not being in touch, and I pretended it was okay. That was 17 years ago.

Before that, we tried every six months or so to navigate the ocean between us, but we never seemed to make it work. I was too hurt, and he was too proud or angry or something else I could never quite understand. We kept drifting apart, and it felt like I was the only one who noticed.

It hurt too much. I was always angry when I thought of him. How do you forgive someone who isn't even sorry they hurt you?

In Matthew, Peter asks Jesus about forgiveness. I picture Peter, looking the Messiah in the eye, questioning Him like a snarky teenager: "Lord, how often should I forgive someone who sins against me? Seven times?"

In all fairness, I don't know if Peter had an attitude. But I know I did. I would be hurt or let down time and again by my father, the person who was supposed to take care of me. In my pain and desperation, I'd go to Jesus asking, "How many times do I need to forgive him? I've already done it so many times. You saw me. I did what I'm supposed to do. How much more do you expect?"

I bet Jesus's response surprised Peter as much as it did me: "'No, not seven times,' Jesus replied, 'but seventy times seven!'"

It turns out Jesus can handle snarky, and He can respond with loving truth. Seven wasn't enough, not even close. He would have us take that seven and multiply it by 70. That's 490.

I don't think 490 is a magic number; rather, Jesus was simply showing us that our forgiveness should far exceed what we may think is fair. The seven times Peter suggested was nothing compared to what is expected of us. Peter and I both thought seven was generous; Jesus has something more extravagant in mind. He wants us to stretch so far beyond our idea of "fair" that it seems ridiculous—490 times more ridiculous.

Is there someone you need to forgive? Someone who hurt you or who keeps hurting you? One and done won't cut it, friend. Forgiveness that reaches the heart requires more from you. But it also gives so much more—more hope, more freedom, more healing—all wrapped up in extravagant forgiveness.

LET'S REFLECT

Is there someone you need to forgive? How do you feel when you think of forgiving extravagantly? Can you start today with just one time?

He Will Help You

For I am the Lord your God who takes hold of your
right hand and says to you, Do not fear; I will help you.

–Isaiah 41:13

Talking about forgiveness can be hard. Sometimes it feels downright impossible. We know the things people have done to us, the things they continue to do. We feel it and walk around with it every day like a heavy weight we drag everywhere we go. The only thing that feels like it will help is justice, fairness. But even that can prove empty.

So what do we do when we feel like we can't forgive? When we feel like we can't do this impossible thing Jesus asked us to do 490 times? When even 490 times isn't enough?

We stop doing it on our own.

I know the world tells us to be strong and that we can do anything. There is some truth to that. But partial worldly truth will never come close to the Truth of God. There are hard things you need to do in this process. Hard things that feel impossible, like forgiving the people who hurt you, those who continue to hurt you, and even forgiving yourself.

The beauty about the hard things God calls us to is that He doesn't call us to do a single one with just our own strength. "So do not fear, for I am with you; do not be dismayed, for I am your God. I will strengthen you and help you; I will uphold you with my righteous right hand" (Isaiah 41:10).

When the idea of forgiveness feels scary, or it feels like you don't have enough strength, God promises to help you and hold you up. You just need to depend on Him to do what He says He will.

Your healing requires work from you. We've seen that as we walk through these days together. Sometimes you will feel weak, but your weakness is not the end. With God, your weakness is the first step to strength, to hope, to healing.

Imagine a young girl trying to pick up a heavy rock. She leans over and wraps her little fingers around it, grunting as she pulls, pushes, and struggles. Maybe you've had past attempts at healing that have felt just like this. (I know I have!)

But then someone comes along, someone much bigger and stronger who wants to see her succeed. That person could pick up the rock all alone and hold it high in the air. The girl would look and see how strong he is. Or that person could say, "Let's do it together." He could grip the rock as the girl puts her little fingers around it. He could lift it just high enough that she could still have her hand on it, still be part of the process. And she would grin and see how strong she is *with his help*.

Friend, God is here saying, "Let's do it together." Are you ready?

LET'S PRAY

Doing this on my own doesn't work, Lord. I'm not strong enough. Show me that You're here, helping me do the hard things. Show me Your strength in my weak places. Amen.

In the Waiting

The Lord is good to those who wait for him,
to the soul who seeks him.

–Lamentations 3:25, ESV

I hit refresh on my phone three times in as many seconds. All I wanted was an update, to know that things were progressing, and for the email I'd been waiting for to load. I wasn't even waiting for anything important, but there's something about waiting that just feels hard.

It's the reason we tap our foot when waiting in line. The reason we push the elevator button again and again. The reason we keep switching lanes in traffic. And it's the reason we rush through the steps we need to take in our healing.

We're tired of waiting. This process doesn't always move at the speed we thought it would. We have visions of what it should look like, a timeline of how long we should be working on it, and a definite longing to just be done with it already. We also compare it to what we see in other people, thinking they did it faster or better.

We want to be complete, to check the box, to be through the hard work. Waiting holds the tension between yesterday and tomorrow, making us watch the clock and rush through the process, all because we want to feel better.

We could talk about the value in seasons (Ecclesiastes 3:1–8), or how waiting builds character (James 5:7–8), but sometimes knowing those things doesn't change how hard it feels. The longing in us can be so deep that we become the kids in the back seat of the family station wagon asking Dad the same questions over and over:

"Are we there yet?"

"How much longer?"

"When will we get there?"

It's natural to want to be through this already, to want to just get to where we desperately long to be: through the emotional heartache to a place of freedom and joy. We simply want to feel better, and the waiting feels like it will never end.

So lean in close and hear this important reminder today: Jesus is with you in the waiting. God is in this place that feels too slow and without hope of ending. This place where you feel in process and vulnerable. This place of not knowing. He is in this place with you.

With God's presence in our waiting, we don't need to keep hitting refresh to see if there is any progress. We can simply let Him be the one to refresh us, even if we're in the exact same place we were yesterday or last week. We can come to Him to help us in this exact moment of waiting for our healing to be complete.

So let's be the kids in the back of the station wagon looking out the window at the scenery, noticing the road, seeing how it feels to ride through this place, and trusting that Dad is driving at exactly the right speed to get us there safely.

LET'S PUT IT INTO PRACTICE

Tell God how you feel about waiting today. Then declare to Him, "I will trust that You are with me in the waiting."

Two Beautiful Words

In all their troubles, he was troubled, too. He didn't
send someone else to help them. He did it himself,
in person. Out of his own love and pity he redeemed
them. He rescued them and carried them
along for a long, long time.

—Isaiah 63:9, MSG

Tucked in Luke is one of my favorite interactions Jesus has with a woman—but it may not be the one you expect.

Jesus always seemed to be talking with people and teaching things along His journeys. This trip to Capernaum and the village of Nain was no different. Only Jesus could enter a town, start with healing and raising someone from the dead, and move on to talking about Old Testament prophecy and correction. He would finally wrap it up with the beautiful story of the woman who was a sinner pouring out the most expensive perfume to honor Jesus. There's so much here that you could miss one of the most loving interactions.

"As he approached the town gate, a dead person was being carried out—the only son of his mother, and she was a widow. And a large crowd from the town was with her" (Luke 7:12).

This woman was grieving. She had lost her husband and now her son. She carried not just sadness but uncertainty. She was likely vulnerable, both socially and economically, since she no longer had someone to care for her. This woman carried her brokenness and burden with every step down that village street with no hope for relief.

But then, Jesus was there. "When the Lord saw her, his heart went out to her and he said, 'Don't cry'" (Luke 7:13).

I can only imagine the depth of compassion Jesus had in those two words. He knew her brokenness fully and went to her to soothe her grieving soul. But He didn't stop there.

"Then he went up and touched the bier they were carrying him on, and the bearers stood still. He said, 'Young man, I say to you, get up!' The dead man sat up and began to talk, and Jesus gave him back to his mother" (Luke 7:14–15).

Another miracle. A life raised from the dead. But it was so much more than that for the widow.

"Jesus gave him back to his mother."

On an ordinary walk in an ordinary village, Jesus showed compassion and gave this woman what she needed to heal her brokenness. He went to her, He comforted her, and He brought hope back into her life.

We all carry broken places in our hearts—places that feel without hope and lonely, places that appear one way on the outside but are even more complex and heavy on the inside. And in those places, we long to be seen, to be loved, and to be cared for.

Jesus saw that widow in Luke, fully and completely, and met her in love the way she needed it most. He enacted what was written in Isaiah hundreds of years before He was even born. The prophesy about the Messiah is seen coming to pass with this widow in Luke, and it can be seen in your life today.

Jesus sees you, fully and completely, and meets you in love the way you need it most. Even on your hardest journey, with the most unknown things in your heart, Jesus meets you with compassion today.

LET'S REFLECT

What broken places do you have in your heart today? Do you believe Jesus has compassion and love for you there? How can you see Him coming to you in that place?

Explore and Discover

Now you've got my feet on the life path, all radiant
from the shining of your face. Ever since you
took my hand, I'm on the right way.

–*Psalm 16:11, MSG*

There is one thing my family always does when we go on vacation. In fact, it's the first thing we do when we arrive. It doesn't matter if it's a hotel or a campsite or a rental property. When we arrive, we always explore our new place.

This exploring isn't travel exploring, like seeing landmarks and finding restaurants (although my husband always has a keen eye for coffee shops nearby, and I tend to find the desserts). This is an exploration of where we are staying, the place we are living in for the next few days.

We want to see if it's really like the pictures, how many bedrooms there are, if the bathroom is clean and pretty. We even open fridges and sliding doors. What does it look like and feel like and sound like in this new place where we've never been before? How can we be at home here, even if just for a little while?

You may feel like you're in a new place lately—that this journey has brought you somewhere new. There may even be an awareness that it is temporary because you know you have more healing ahead. No matter how long you've been here or how long you'll stay, give yourself permission to explore.

Look at how things feel for you. Think about how your days look and what you get done. Delight in the unexpected joy, even with the lingering sorrow. Discover how you've changed and what that feels like in your body, in your soul. Check out the fresh hope sprouting in fields you thought were barren.

You have permission to explore with a childlike hope, ready to see the beautiful new things all around you. Does that scare you? Does it feel premature to explore with hope when you know you're not done yet?

God knows exactly where you are today. He knows where you were and how far you have to go. And still He's longing for you to explore exactly where you are now. It is only in the exploration that you discover the unexpected: He is not waiting for you to complete your healing to show you the depth of His love for you.

The fullness of God's love and grace is here, ready to explore, right in the middle of your journey. You have permission to look around, to hope, and to dream, even without being done. Don't wait, friend. Experience and discover the fullness of God in this new place.

LET'S PUT IT INTO PRACTICE

List three things about the new place you're in on your healing journey, and celebrate them today.

I Thought
I Was Done

> Before Isaiah had left the middle court, the word
> of the Lord came to him: "Go back and tell Hezekiah,
> the ruler of my people, 'This is what the Lord, the God
> of your father David, says: I have heard your prayer
> and seen your tears; I will heal you.'"
>
> *−2 Kings 20:4–5*

When you take time to explore the new place you're in, it can feel pretty great. In fact, you may look around and see the progress you've made, the hope you're discovering, and think you've arrived. Maybe you even want to set up camp here permanently.

Wouldn't it be nice to be done?

Before you unpack your bags and call someone to send the rest of your things, there's a bit of tough love you need to hear right now. I'm certain today is the day you need it because you're far enough along. Plus, God always has a way of timing these things so we discover them at the moment we need them most.

Are you ready? Take a deep breath, friend, and know I'm saying this in love. YOU'RE NOT DONE YET. Yes, it looks like I'm yelling, but I promise I'm not. This is my way of putting my hands on your shoulders and looking you straight in the eye as I tell you the truth.

This new place you're in may feel great, like you've made so much progress and hope is dwelling in you. It may feel comfortable and even look pretty nice. Or maybe it feels like you've gotten nowhere—like these past days you've taken the tiniest of baby steps and have lost hope of ever getting where you want to be. Like it's a lost cause, so you'll just settle in comfortably here.

But you're not done yet. This is a journey. And when you're on a journey, you need to keep going. You know what you're moving toward. You know exactly what you want: to walk fully in your healing. It isn't easy to make the whole journey to get there. But you have this promise: "So keep a firm grip on the faith. The suffering won't last forever. It won't be long before this generous God who has great plans for us in Christ—eternal and glorious plans they are!—will have you put together and on your feet for good. He gets the last word; yes, he does" (1 Peter 5:9–10, MSG).

And you know you're not there yet. So, friend, imagine me taking your hand. We can turn our full selves to face the road ahead and take the next step, followed by another and another and another, until we are exactly where God wants us to be.

I know sometimes it feels hard to keep going. I know comfortable feels safe and easy. But God has good things for you in this moment and in the moments to come. You just can't see them because you're not there yet.

Keep going.

LET'S PRAY

Lord, help me keep going. When I get comfortable and don't want to press on; when I feel afraid and can't see the way ahead; when I don't see my progress and want to give up, help me keep going, confident that You hear my prayer and will heal me. Amen.

On the Cusp

I am convinced that any suffering we endure is less than nothing compared to the magnitude of glory that is about to be unveiled within us.

–*Romans 8:18, TPT*

Do you know you are a daughter of God? I'm not talking about the Sunday school answer or the nod and smile while you secretly dismiss the idea. No, I'm talking about for real, deep in your bones. You are a daughter of God, a coheir with Christ, even in this unfinished place.

You need to know who you are to believe what God has for you. Paul knew that. He had walked through his own transformation with God, so he had firsthand experience. In his letter to the Romans, Paul was teaching believers like you and me so that we could fully understand and live in the Truth.

"For the Holy Spirit makes God's fatherhood real to us as he whispers into our innermost being, 'You are God's beloved child!'" (Romans 8:16, TPT). The Holy Spirit living in you whispers this today. You are His child. And not only that, you are beloved. Isn't that amazing?

But what about when it doesn't feel amazing? What about times when you are struggling with fear or suffering and you can't quite grasp this idea that you are His beloved child?

Paul talks a lot about who we are before he gets to that. He reminds us:

- "You did not receive the 'spirit of religious duty,' leading you back into the fear *of never being good enough*" (Romans 8:15, TPT).

- "You have received the 'Spirit of full acceptance,' enfolding you into the family of God" (Romans 8:15, TPT).

- "And since we are his true children, we qualify to share all his treasures, for indeed, we are heirs of God himself" (Romans 8:17, TPT).

Paul didn't forget about the hard parts, either. In fact, he prepares you for them: "We will experience being co-glorified with him provided that we accept his sufferings as our own" (Romans 8:17, TPT).

The suffering is part of the package. It's not because God doesn't love you and not because you deserve it—no. The suffering is simply part of existing as a human, and some of it is because you are walking with God. There is not one thing you can do to change that. But there is something you can do to get through it. There is something for you beyond the suffering. Remember Paul's words: "I am convinced that any suffering we endure is less than nothing compared to the magnitude of glory that is about to be unveiled within us."

There is glory on the other side of your suffering. And you're close, so close, to seeing it and watching that glory that lives in you be unveiled by the One who loves you more than any other. These aren't just Sunday school lesson words. No, friend. They're real.

You are on the cusp of glory. Keep going. God is about to do something amazing.

LET'S PUT IT INTO PRACTICE

Say these words aloud: "I am convinced that any suffering I endure is less than nothing compared to the magnitude of glory that is about to be unveiled within me. I am God's beloved child!"

The Thoughts Keep Coming Back

Search me, God, and know my heart;
test me and know my anxious thoughts.
See if there is any offensive way in me,
and lead me in the way everlasting.

–Psalm 139:23–24

I spent years of my life believing that I wasn't good enough, that I wasn't pretty enough, that I would never be enough to make someone stay. Thoughts like those were part of everything I did, and I don't even know how they got there.

When we believe something about ourselves long enough, it becomes part of who we are. Maybe that's why the old whisper snuck into my mind so easily the other day: "You're not enough."

The words were familiar. No one ever said them directly to me, but still the idea took root—from things that happened, things I saw, things I lost. "You're not enough." The thought became like a soundtrack playing constantly in the background. I listened to thoughts like these for most of my life, believing them instead of Truth.

I tried everything I could think of to fight off these ideas, but they always came back. After years of trying, I was so tired that I finally gave up. I thought, *I can't do it. I can't fight these negative thoughts. They always come back. It's useless.*

In that surrender, I discovered I was right. I couldn't do it.

David struggled with this tug-of-war, too. He knew who God created him to be, but he struggled with his thoughts that didn't align with that. In Psalm 139, he writes about how intimately God knows him, even from before he was born. And still he didn't know what to do with his negative thoughts, so he asked God for help.

"Search me, God," he prayed. But he didn't end there. He asked God for help: "lead me in the everlasting way."

Do you ever have negative thoughts that seem to keep playing over and over? You don't need to struggle with them on your own. You can go to God, and ask Him to search your heart and mind for anything that doesn't align with the love and grace of God. God longs for us to know and believe the Truth deep inside.

And just like David, you don't need to stop there. God goes beyond putting a spotlight on the negative things we believe. He comes in love, wanting to gently lead us to a place where we can confidently believe in His love, His grace, and His Word.

God knows our struggle with thoughts that don't align with Truth. And He wants to help us in the tender, merciful way that only He can. Let's ask for His help today.

LET'S PRAY

Lord, I am so tired of struggling with negative thoughts. I can't fight them on my own. I need Your help. Search me and reveal my thoughts. Then, in Your grace, lead me to Your Truth about who I am. Amen.

You're So Close

As for us, we have all of these great witnesses who
encircle us like clouds. So we must let go of every
wound that has pierced us and the sin we so easily fall
into. Then we will be able to run life's marathon race
with passion and determination, for the path has been
already marked out before us.

–Hebrews 12:1, TPT

In every race, there is a point when you feel like giving up. You look
back and the starting line is so far behind you that you can't even make
it out, but you also can't see the finish line so far ahead. It feels like
you're going to be running forever. You're not even sure you can reach
the end.

We long for the moment when we run through the ribbon at the
finish line. I can picture that moment for myself. I'd have my hands
raised high over my head, a broad smile across my face, and confetti
falling down around me (because life feels more fun with confetti).
People would cheer, and I would know that I had finished the race
strong. I would feel like a winner.

But sometimes that moment feels so far away. I wonder if I will ever
get there. It feels like the cheering crowd has given up and gone home.
Who will throw the confetti? It feels like I've failed before I've even
finished.

Giving up feels easier when you can't see the finish line. Before you
stop, though, just listen. Listen to what God reminds us:

"As for us, we have all of these great witnesses who encircle us like
clouds." This verse is about us. And we're not in it alone. We have witnesses cheering us on in our race—heavenly witnesses.

"So we must let go of every wound that has pierced us and the sin we so easily fall into." In other words, we just need to let go of the things that hurt and the mistakes we make.

"Then we will be able to run life's marathon race with passion and determination, for the path has been already marked out before us." God has marked and cleared the path for us. We just need to follow it.

When you feel like you can't go one more step, remember this promise. You are not alone, and you are running the race God has marked out for you. Even when you want to give up, you can let that feeling go and run your race. You just have to keep going. You are so close, my friend. You are so very close.

LET'S REFLECT

What does the finish line of this race look like for you? What are the things that trip you up and make you want to quit? How can you keep going?

Take the Leap

With the arrival of Jesus, the Messiah, that fateful
dilemma is resolved. Those who enter into Christ's
being-here-for-us no longer have to live under a
continuous, low-lying black cloud. A new power is
in operation. The Spirit of life in Christ, like a strong
wind, has magnificently cleared the air, freeing
you from a fated lifetime of brutal tyranny
at the hands of sin and death.

–Romans 8:1–2, MSG

I wasn't sure I could take the leap. The pier stood 10 feet above the cold
Maine water, but it felt more like 50. My family had come down here
every day of our vacation to do this—to simply jump in the water. Each
day I would stand safely on the pier, taking pictures and videos for
them. But deep inside I wanted to be brave enough to jump.

By our last day, I finally decided I would do it. When we went to
the pier, I handed the camera to my youngest and walked to the edge.
I had prepared myself for this all day, and it was my last chance before
we left. I was ready. I was excited. Yet when I stood there and stared at
the water, the doubt crept in. *You haven't been able to do it all week. What
makes you think you can do it now?*

I stepped back for a moment, staring at the dark water. My old way
of thinking told me I couldn't. *It's too hard. It's too high. It's too scary.* But
I had decided I would. I had a new way of thinking that declared in
faith that I could do the hard thing in front of me. Which thought would
I listen to?

In your healing journey, you're standing on the edge between your
old thinking and this new way of thinking you've been investing in,

believing, and working toward. You may have old doubts creeping in, pulling you back from the healing into the familiar safety of what was.

My friend, God did not give you this moment to focus on what was. He gave you this very moment in your journey to focus on what is. You're no longer trapped in the dilemma of whether it will work or whether God will be faithful in this place. God will be faithful.

It helps to reflect on Paul's words in Romans: "Those who enter into Christ's being-here-for-us no longer have to live under a continuous, low-lying black cloud. A new power is in operation." No matter what your doubts tell you, there is a new power within you.

"The Spirit of life in Christ, like a strong wind, has magnificently cleared the air, freeing you from a fated lifetime of brutal tyranny at the hands of sin and death." The Spirit has cleared the way from pain to a life of healing and hope. Your doubts cannot hold you in tyranny any longer. Your way is clear and free.

No matter what doubts you feel, you can step forward, fully ready to leap in. When you do, those doubts are washed away and you are free.

LET'S PUT IT INTO PRACTICE

Picture yourself on the edge of that pier, longing to leap into the ocean. Notice the doubts that hold you back. Take a deep breath and declare, "My doubts cannot hold me back! The Spirit has cleared the way for me!"

Then I Am Strong

"My grace is sufficient for you, for my power is made perfect in weakness." Therefore I will boast all the more gladly about my weaknesses, so that Christ's power may rest on me.

−2 Corinthians 12:9

Have you ever had a tiny splinter or a thorn in your skin? Even the smallest sliver can cause pain. Paul knew that feeling well, and he has a challenge for us.

Paul saw God move in ways few people did in biblical times. In 2 Corinthians 12, Paul experienced something that is hard to fully understand today. He describes that God wanted to keep him focused, so he was given a thorn in his flesh. When I think of a thorn, I think about something from a rosebush or a briar. But Paul describes this thorn as a messenger from Satan sent to torment him.

Here was a man who was walking with God and interacting with the Holy Spirit in ways that still amaze us today, and he was given something to torment him. It seems rather harsh. But God had good reason. And Paul recognized it—eventually.

First, he asked God to take it away—not once but three times. That sounds like the biblical equivalent of begging. Have you ever begged God to take away a thorn in your life? I know I have!

But God did not. Instead, God showed Paul the value in this weak spot in his life: "My grace is sufficient for you, for my power is made perfect in weakness." God clearly instructed Paul that this thorn, this weak area he is dealing with, cleared the way for God's perfect power in Paul's life.

And Paul responded, "Therefore I will boast all the more gladly about my weaknesses, so that Christ's power may rest on me. That is why, for Christ's sake, I delight in weaknesses, in insults, in hardships, in persecutions, in difficulties. For when I am weak, then I am strong" (2 Corinthians 12:9–10).

There is no text written between God telling Paul that his weakness is a good thing and Paul's choice to believe it, to boast of it even. I know I would have quite the back-and-forth with God, probably even begging for Him again to take the weakness away so I could be strong. But God's ways don't always fit into our logic.

God declared the benefit of weakness, and Paul accepted it fully. God wants the same for us. We don't need to rid ourselves of our weak areas, the thorns that we can't seem to pick out. Those are the places where God's strength and glory will show the greatest.

It may not feel easy, but you can choose to find joy in your weakness, resting on the promise that God's perfect strength will show in those places. Your weakness can be your strength!

LET'S PRAY

Lord, help me trust You to come in grace and bring Your perfect strength into those areas where I am experiencing difficulty. Help me find joy in my challenges because I can celebrate Your strength. Amen.

Believe, Then See

Before the spies lay down for the night, she went up
on the roof and said to them, "I know that the Lord
has given you this land."

—Joshua 2:8–9

Rahab was a woman known for an act of great bravery. When her community was at risk, she hid two spies who were coming for intel. She protected them, and, when the time came, they protected her. You can read the whole story in Joshua. But my favorite thing about Rahab was her faith.

She believed in something that hadn't happened yet. She believed it so deeply that she risked her life. She risked her family's lives, too. It may sound foolish, but somewhere deep inside, she had a belief that outweighed every fear, every doubt, every logical reason. She believed before she saw it happen.

When Rahab hid the spies on her roof, she had full faith that their army would defeat her community. She didn't know these men. She didn't even know their faith fully. Yet she believed in them because of God.

There wasn't even a war yet. There hadn't been a major attack in her city. There were rumors of it. People were concerned. But nothing had happened except a few spies coming for intel. Yet she knew what she believed: "I know that the Lord has given you this land." She declared and acted on her beliefs before she saw any proof.

What if you were brave like Rahab? You've spent weeks reading about God's promises for your healing and freedom. Maybe you're even feeling that in areas of your life. But do you believe it in the areas you're still working on? Do you believe in your healing before you see it?

Be brave and have the deep faith that Rahab modeled for you. Make a choice to believe in the healing that is yet to come. You don't have to feel it. It doesn't even have to fully make sense. But you can choose to have faith before you see the fruit.

In the New Testament, Thomas wasn't sure about Jesus's resurrected body. Jesus didn't condemn Thomas for his doubts; Jesus welcomed them: "Then he said to Thomas, 'Put your finger here; see my hands. Reach out your hand and put it into my side. Stop doubting and believe'" (John 20:27).

It's a truly beautiful act of love from Jesus—an act of love that He offers us with every one of our doubts. But when Thomas did this and believed, Jesus continued: "'Because you have seen me, you have believed; blessed are those who have not seen and yet have believed'" (John 20:29).

Jesus will never condemn you for doubts you bring to Him. But He recognizes there is something special that happens when we have faith in the things we have yet to see—faith like Rahab's, faith to believe in all of God's promises for your healing, even though it is not yet complete.

There will be times we are like Thomas, times we need proof from God. But let there also be times we are women like Rahab, women who believe before we see. Women who believe the promise before we have proof.

LET'S PUT IT INTO PRACTICE

Tell God that you believe His promises for your healing, even if they are not yet complete. Say aloud, "God, I believe in the healing You promise me."

Is God Hiding?

You will seek me and find me when you
seek me with all your heart.

–Jeremiah 29:13

I remember walking through the cool church basement, my eyes alert as I looked behind little plastic chairs and bulletin boards leaning against the wall for any sign of the other kids. Everything was eerily quiet, except for the sound of my footsteps and me talking to myself to make things a little less creepy.

"Come out, come out, wherever you are!" It always sounded more like a plea than a chant from a game of hide-and-seek. I always imagined the other kids were snickering with a hand pressed hard over their mouths as they heard me come near, then eventually pass by. No matter how hard I looked, it always felt as if I was seeking longer than anyone else, as if I would never find anyone and I would just be seeking forever (or at least until my mom came to get me).

Sometimes it can feel as if we're playing a game of hide-and-seek with God. As if we are searching for Him around every corner, tiptoeing through our days wondering when (if ever) we will find Him, especially when it comes to our healing.

We look through our past, wondering where He was, how He allowed things to happen, why we felt so alone. We stare at our present, thinking about all the possibilities, challenged by the pull of our hurt and the hope of healing. We gaze into the future, curious about what could be, wondering if healing is real and, more importantly, if it's real for us.

We ask questions of ourselves, of our souls. Is God really here? Why does it feel so hard to find Him? Is He playing hide-and-seek with me?

But God is not like kids playing hide-and-seek. He is never trying to stay hidden from us. God is so full of love for us that He longs for us to seek Him and find Him. Even back thousands of years ago He promised: "You will seek me *and find me* when you seek me with all your heart" (emphasis mine).

It's no surprise that we need to seek God. He knew we would have to look for Him. But did you see what He promised? We *will* find Him. It's certain. The only catch? We need to seek Him with our whole heart.

In your healing journey, you are probably working on so many things. But the most important, and the most fruitful, will always be to seek God with your whole heart. More than answers, more than understanding, more even than the healing, seek God.

This isn't a game of hide-and-seek played in the church basement. This is a promise. When you seek Him, you will find the healing you long for.

LET'S REFLECT

How do you feel when you can't find God? Do you think He's hiding from you? How does the promise in Jeremiah encourage you?

When You Pray

Therefore I tell you, whatever you ask for in prayer,
believe that you have received it, and it will be yours.

—Mark 11:24

Prayer is one of your best healing tools. It may sound obvious; you may even be tempted to think, *I know this,* and skip this devotion. But sometimes the most basic parts of our faith are the ones we need the most help with.

In your journey through this devotional, you've spent time in the Word, you've been encouraged, you've thought, and you've prayed. But have you prayed *and believed?* Have you really believed that God would not only hear your prayers but answer them?

One day when Jesus and His disciples left Jerusalem, Peter saw that something Jesus said had come to pass. The night before Jesus had cursed a fruitless fig tree. It looked strong and healthy but wasn't producing fruit. And that next morning Peter noticed that the tree had withered and died.

Instead of being amazed, Jesus decided to teach about the power He gives us with our prayers. "'Have faith in God,' Jesus answered. 'Truly I tell you, if anyone says to this mountain, 'Go, throw yourself into the sea,' and does not doubt in their heart but believes that what they say will happen, it will be done for them'" (Mark 11:22–23).

Believe that what you ask of God will be done if it is in His will. God's will is for you to experience His love and healing—always. It's why Jesus died. It's why He rose. It's why you have help here on earth and a promise of eternity in heaven. Knowing this and believing it enables you to pray powerful prayers!

When you pray for your healing, you can believe it will happen. Believe God will work in your heart and soul to repair those wounded places with gentleness and mercy so you can have freedom. Your prayers are powerful. Not because of fancy words, but because of your faith in the One who hears them.

Jesus continued: "Therefore I tell you, whatever you ask for in prayer, believe that you have received it, and it will be yours."

You know (or you're learning) that God hears you. He listens to everything you say and think and feel. Now is the time to start believing that the things you ask for in Him will come to pass. Your healing, your wholeness, your hope for a future are all part of His best promise for you.

He wants you to ask for healing in confidence that He will do it. Pray believing it is true, and see what God does!

LET'S PUT IT INTO PRACTICE

Whenever you need to, find a moment to sit and reflect on your healing journey. Ask God to heal you, and tell Him you believe He will!

Tell Him You Don't Believe

"'If you can'?" said Jesus. "Everything is possible for one who believes." Immediately the boy's father exclaimed, "I do believe; help me overcome my unbelief!"

—Mark 9:23–24

I always love stories in the Bible of people I can relate to. Stories that show vulnerability and humanity help me feel seen and understood. One of the best examples is of a nameless man who comes to Jesus in desperation. I can relate to feeling both nameless and desperate at times. But watch what Jesus does with nameless and desperate people.

Mark describes a man who sought Jesus because his son was possessed by a spirit. The desperate father explains what his son is experiencing: inability to speak, lack of body control, and seizure-like episodes. The description is straightforward and honest, withholding nothing from Jesus.

And then the father explains that he brought his son to the disciples for healing, but they couldn't do it. I can picture the defeat in the father's eyes, the way his shoulders drop and his eyes fill with tears. When Jesus asks to see the boy, He witnesses what the father describes and listens to even more heartbreaking effects of this boy's struggle, followed by another plea from the father: "But if you can do anything, take pity on us and help us" (Mark 9:22).

"'"If you can"?' said Jesus. 'Everything is possible for one who believes.'"

And then comes the moment where I feel the deep connection to this father, this man desperately longing and begging for help:

"Immediately the boy's father exclaimed, 'I do believe; help me overcome my unbelief!'"

Did you catch that? He declared both his belief and his need for God to help him believe. He didn't pretend he could do it on his own. He had faith, but he knew he needed help to fully believe.

Can you imagine standing next to this man, holding your breath to see what Jesus would do with this desperate plea, this faith and lack of faith all jumbled together? Would Jesus honor this vulnerability or correct it? What would happen to the father? To the boy?

To put it simply, Jesus healed the boy. Jesus honored the father's heart, too—both the strong parts and the weak parts—because the father came to Jesus with all of it.

God does that for you, as well. You can come to Him with your declaration of faith as well as your plea for help to have faith. You can believe and ask for help believing. It may not make sense, especially in a world of self-sufficiency. But Jesus is ready to help you believe. He did it for the father, healing his son, and He will do it for you!

LET'S PRAY

Lord, my prayer today is simple. I believe. Help me overcome my unbelief! Amen.

Reach for Your Healing

For the Spirit God gave us does not make us timid,
but gives us power, love and self-discipline.

–2 Timothy 1:7

Walking through the long grass, I was glad I wore my sneakers on our annual trip to the apple orchard. I am always tempted to wear some cute, Instagram-worthy outfit, but with three kids and the reality of an orchard, sneakers and jeans are always the best bet.

Apples dangled from trees all around us, and the only question was which ones to pick. My youngest didn't take long to decide. As her gaze drifted up, she pointed to the perfect apple. I tried to follow her eyes and her finger to see which one it was. It wasn't the low-hanging ones she could reach. It was up much farther, higher than her hands, higher than my hands, higher than our heads. She wanted the one right near the top of the tree. There was no way she could reach it, and no way I could reach it.

That's when her dad came and hoisted her up to sit on his shoulders. She giggled, and I grabbed the camera. As I watched them, her hand reached up, but it still wasn't high enough. So she shifted, standing on his shoulders instead of sitting. She gained hope in that moment as much as she gained inches. I watched her little hand reach, reach, reach as her dad held her legs, and I abandoned the camera to stand behind them, ready to catch her.

She never fell. Instead, she reached up, grabbed the apple, and shouted, "I did it!" We all cheered and smiled at her accomplishment.

Healing Devotional for Women

Your healing is that apple. You may not be able to reach it on your own, but you do have help. Your Heavenly Father is coming up, holding you, lifting you to reach for it. He doesn't falter, and He won't let you go. When you stand on His shoulders, your healing is right there.

It may feel scary to reach for it. It's normal to feel uncertain. But God is neither scary nor uncertain, and He is the one holding you up. He is the one lifting you to reach with the confidence of a child on her daddy's shoulders. No matter what you've experienced with your earthly dad, God is the Father you can rely on.

His Spirit lives in you, giving you the power you need, the love of a Father, and the inspiration and courage to follow through. He's got you. You just need to reach.

LET'S REFLECT

Do you believe God is lifting you up, giving you all you need to reach for your healing? What holds you back? What gives you the courage to reach?

The Circle Within You

If anyone acknowledges that Jesus is the Son of
God, God lives in them and they in God. And so we
know and rely on the love God has for us. God is love.
Whoever lives in love lives in God, and God in them.

−1 John 4:15−16

It's easy on this healing journey to get wrapped up in hard things. After all, emotional healing stems from an emotional wound. We have spent these past weeks working on our struggles, our hang-ups, our challenges, and even our sins. Although we are walking in more freedom than we were at the beginning of this book, it hasn't been easy getting here. That's why we need to remember who God is more than ever: "God is love." I know that sounds simple—which is a far cry from how we might feel emotionally. But it is the truest thing about who God is. And more than that, "If anyone acknowledges that Jesus is the Son of God, God lives in them and they in God."

Do you know what this means for you? Love lives in you—not romantic love, not human love, but Love. The very essence of who God is lives inside of you because you are one who believes in Him—not one who is perfect, not one who is without scars, but simply one who believes.

I know that can feel hard to understand, especially as someone who has experienced worldly love that is flawed, imperfect, and sometimes even painful. Experiences like mine with someone who was supposed to love you faithfully may even be part of the healing you're working so hard on.

But God's love is different. And it is full of good things for you—always. Remember, "We know and rely on the love God has for us."

God's love is dependable. You can rely on it today in your healing, in your pain, and in your hope for a future. There is no time that God's love has left you. No time that you've driven God's love away. No time that you were without the deep, perfect, abiding love of God. As one who believes in Him, you are filled with His love.

There may be times you fear His love isn't there. Even after you've walked through your healing, you may doubt or worry. But fear, doubt, and worry are not part of who God is. "There is no fear in love. But perfect love drives out fear" (1 John 4:18).

Let God, in His perfect love, drive out any fear left in you. Invite Him to fill you and show you His love, so deep that you can't help but believe it.

All you need to do is acknowledge that God lives in you and you live in God. In that simple act, you declare that love—true, perfect love—lives within you.

LET'S PUT IT INTO PRACTICE

Take a deep breath, and imagine the beautiful, perfect love of God living inside you. Think about what it feels like as you breathe in and out, remembering that the Spirit of God inhabits you and fills you with His perfect love. Picture it going around, never ending. That is what you carry inside you.

Just Come Near

Come near to God and he will come near to you.

—James 4:8

I stood next to the hospital bed. Everything around me felt foreign and cold. Wires were draped everywhere, machines beeped, and bags of fluid hung and dripped. None of it felt like the warm grandma I knew.

Yet, there she lay. I saw her with my own eyes, and I knew it was her. I recognized her beautiful hands, with all their freckles and age spots, more than I recognized her face. There was nothing wrong with her face, but she wasn't awake, and I missed her broad smile. I longed to hear her laugh and feel her wrap me in a deep hug. Instead, I would have to settle for resting my hand on hers.

I longed for her to reach for my hand with all the love she carried. I knew if she could, she certainly would. She was there, but she was no longer herself.

Sometimes when we approach God, it can feel like my grandma's hospital room. We wonder if we should be there. We wonder if He sees us. We wonder, if we reach out, can He reach back?

We don't have to wonder.

James was Jesus's brother. He knew Jesus, but He didn't believe who Jesus was until after His resurrection. Imagine, he knew Jesus his whole life, but never really knew Him until after He died. I think we can all relate to James in some ways—the knowing yet not knowing, both at the same time.

And that is why we wonder. We wonder, when we come to Him, if He will indeed meet us. James, this kindred spirit, tells us, "Come near to God and he will come near to you."

There is no pretense and no uncertainty. It's simple and beautiful and for you today. You don't need to wonder if God will meet you. You don't need to worry that He won't show up or that He'll make you do it all on your own. Simply come near to Him, and He comes near to you.

In your pursuit of healing, this promise still stands. When you are ready, full of vigor and excitement about your healing, come near to Him, and He comes near to you. When you are in a hard place, weary from the work of healing, come near to Him, and He comes near to you. When you are uncertain, wondering if you are getting anywhere, come near to Him, and He comes near to you. And when you are full of joy, discovering the freedom and hope He gives, come near to Him, and He comes near to you.

You never have to worry if He will come. He is a sure thing. Just come near, and He will be there to meet you.

LET'S PRAY

Lord, I come near to You today. Show me that You are here, that You meet me in this place. Show me that You will always meet me every time I come to You. Amen.

God Makes a Way

Stop dwelling on the past. Don't even remember
these former things. I am doing something brand
new, *something unheard of.* Even now it sprouts
and grows and matures. Don't you perceive it?
I will make a way in the wilderness and open
up flowing streams in the desert.

–Isaiah 43:18–19, TPT

Even Bible heroes needed reminders of God's faithfulness. Can you believe it? Greats like Moses and Isaiah, Paul and David, Mary and Rahab. Even the nation of Israel, the one God protected and provided for with great miracles, needed to be reminded. They all needed reminders of who God was and who He would be.

In Isaiah, we find some beautiful scriptures reminding us of who God is and the hope He brings. But even more than that, we are given specific instructions about moving forward: "Stop dwelling on the past. Don't even remember these former things."

Friend, we can spend a lot of time in the past. We can look at it and dissect it. We can learn from it and protect its memories. And while there is a season for that, a time when it is good for us to consider what happened then, it is not a place for us to dwell.

God doesn't want you to focus on the past because of what He's doing now. "I am doing something brand new, something unheard of."

Imagine, for a moment, the idea of something new. Hold on to that. Think about it: something new and different from your past.

The same God of great miracles, like parting the sea and raising the dead, is showing you how to move forward. You can stop focusing on the past, not because it didn't happen or it doesn't matter. You can stop focusing on the past because God, the God of miracles, is doing something new in you.

Isaiah says, "Even now it sprouts and grows and matures. Don't you perceive it? I will make a way in the wilderness and open up flowing streams in the desert."

Right now there is something sprouting, growing, maturing in the place where you thought the land was barren, in the place where you didn't see a way (and maybe you still don't). But God does. He sees what is happening right now—not because of you, but because of Him.

Your healing is growing in the desert places of your heart because God is full of love and mercy for you. "Don't you perceive it?" Your job isn't to make it happen. Your task is to look for it, to stop living in yesterday, and to believe what God is doing today.

God makes a way—even in the most impossible places, God makes a way.

LET'S PUT IT INTO PRACTICE

Write today's verses down as an act of faith that God is indeed making a way in your former wilderness.

It Is Done

He himself bore our sins in his body on the tree, that
we might die to sin and live to righteousness. By his
wounds you have been healed.

–1 Peter 2:24, ESV

The rain fell steadily for days. Every time I looked out the window, I hoped to see the sun break through the clouds. I longed for its warmth on my face.

It's not that I don't like the rain. Quite the opposite, actually. I love a rainy day when I can stay home and be cozy. The sound of rain falling on the roof is one of my favorite things, especially at night as I fall asleep.

But there had been days of clouds and rain, days without hope of seeing the sun, and days of needing a little brightness in my life. As much as I loved the rain, I missed the blue sky and sunshine.

Even so, I knew the change would come. Even though the forecast was uncertain, even though there wasn't even a hint of blue in the sky, I knew the clouds would clear and I would see the sun. I had full confidence in something I couldn't see.

The day Jesus died on the cross, He wanted you to have the same full confidence. His death didn't take away the possibility for rain in your life. It didn't take away the likelihood that you would face storms. I'll let go of the metaphors and state it clearly: It didn't take away every pain or hardship you would experience. But it did create something you could be sure of: healing.

In 1 Peter, you are reminded exactly what His death did for you. His wounds, His pain, His crucifixion, they all brought your healing.

"By his wounds you have been healed." Look at those words. They don't say you might be healed. They don't even say you *will be* healed.

They say you *have been* healed. Past tense. His death gave you the healing you long for.

It may be hard to believe that when you still feel pain or sorrow or fear. It's hard to believe the sun will come out when all we see are clouds. But, friend, keep your eyes to the sky; the sun is coming again.

That day, thousands of years ago, Jesus completed what your heart longs for today. He created a way for you to live in righteousness—no matter what your past is, no matter what you carry with you today, and no matter what you will do in the future. You can live in His righteousness, fully and completely. It's a done deal.

How can you know for sure? God said so. Years and years ago God used someone to write the words you need to hear today. You are healed in Him. Now it's time to believe it!

LET'S REFLECT

How do you feel when you read the words *you have been healed*? What is one way you can live today, believing in the healing God gave you?

Go in Courage

"Be strong and courageous. Do not be afraid or
terrified because of them, for the Lord your God goes
with you; he will never leave you nor forsake you."

—Deuteronomy 31:6

It's hard to believe we're at the end of our journey together. You have worked so hard and come so far. You have sought God and the healing He so lovingly gives—the healing you longed for, the healing you prayed for.

Maybe you feel like your journey is done—something amazing you've completed. The end of a journey can be exciting, like we've checked something off our list. Or maybe you feel there's still more to do. Although you have come so far, you still see the road ahead you need to keep walking.

No matter what you've completed or what you've yet to do, no matter where you are, this is less an end and more of a launch. God has so much more for you to go through, to *grow* through.

Consider this your commissioning. We don't use that word often in today's world, but it's the best way to describe what's to come for you. *Commission* means to be ready and appointed to do something, to be sent forth to move forward. And you are going forward.

You're stepping into a new place filled with hope and perhaps a little uncertainty. It's easy to fall into worry about what's ahead. Wouldn't it be nicer to think about how far you've come? Yes, I'm sure it would. And you have come so very far, but you have nothing to worry about what is to come.

Listen to the words of Moses: "'Be strong and courageous. Do not be afraid or terrified because of them, for the Lord your God goes with you; he will never leave you nor forsake you.'"

You can be strong; you can move forward in freedom and joy, facing whatever is to come, because God goes with you. He won't leave when things get tough. He won't back out of the joy and hope He has promised you. He goes with you today.

Hearing this once may not be enough. Moses knew Joshua would need a reminder for the Promised Land he was about to enter, so he continued: "'The Lord himself goes before you and will be with you; he will never leave you nor forsake you. Do not be afraid; do not be discouraged'" (Deuteronomy 31:8).

This promise is for you as you enter your new land. It is for you as you walk forward from a new place in your healing. The Lord goes before you. The Lord is with you. He will never leave you. He will never forsake you.

You do not have to be afraid or discouraged or worried. God keeps His promises. He kept them then, and He keeps them now.

Walk forward, my friend. Walk forward in your healing!

LET'S PRAY

Lord, I will not be afraid or discouraged. I trust that You go before me and You are with me, never leaving me or turning Your back on me. I trust You, and I will walk forward with You in my healing. Amen.

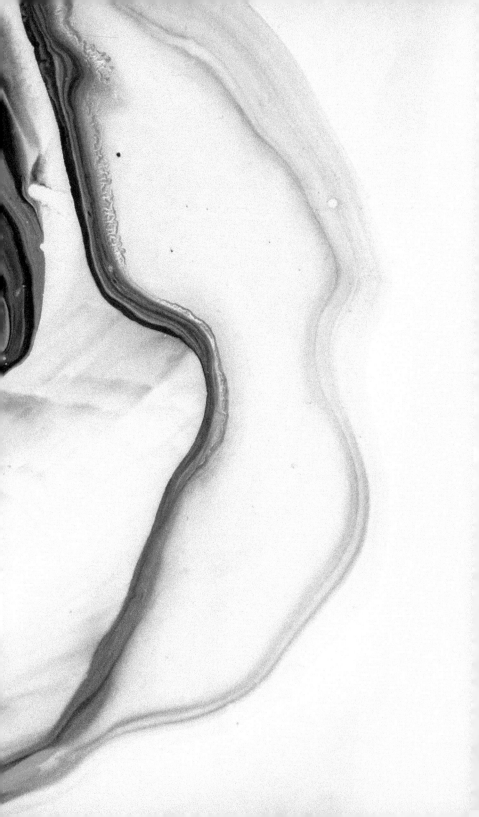

RESOURCES FOR YOUR HEALING JOURNEY

WEBSITES

Better Help
BetterHelp.com
Online counseling from licensed and experienced professionals with a variety of specialties.

Christian Counselor Directory
ChristianCounselorDirectory.com
Online location-based directory offering help finding professional Christian counselors and churches.

Faithful Counseling
FaithfulCounseling.com
Licensed Christian therapists providing online biblically based counseling.

BOOKS

Hastings, Rebecca. *Worthy*. CreateSpace Independent Publishing Platform, 2017.
A 20-day devotional to help you believe the truths God says about you so you can walk forward in your healing.

ACKNOWLEDGMENTS

To everyone who helped get this book into the world, you are part of anything good that comes from these words.

My editors Adrian and Beth, the team at Callisto, and my family and friends, I am so grateful.

Eliza, Timothy, and Annalise, your willingness to give up part of our summer and resist the urge to knock on the door when I was writing did not go unnoticed. You are the best gifts I could ask for. I love you always.

Andrew, you walk with me through my healing every day. And you give me chocolate. I am truly blessed to be your wife. I love you.

And to the Father, who continues to heal me in tender grace and love.

ABOUT THE AUTHOR

 **Rebecca Hastings** believes in finding extraordinary grace in ordinary life. As a writer and speaker, she encourages people to look beyond Sunday morning to discover faith every day. She is the author of *Worthy: Believe Who God Says You Are* and *Daily Meditations for Christians*. Living in Connecticut with her husband, three kids, and two dogs, Rebecca can often be found typing words, driving her kids places, or wherever there is chocolate. Connect with her at RebeccaHastings.net or on Instagram at @MyInkDance.

CPSIA information can be obtained
at www.ICGtesting.com
Printed in the USA
JSHW030516150322
23789JS00003B/3